Critical Acclaim for *Med*

Make a positive impact on your en influence and in your own way while striving to "make the world a better place", " Meditations of an Army Ranger" takes hard earned combat experience, marries it with the classic teachings from past leaders and scholars proposing a practical philosophy to thoughtfully meet the demands of today's globalized world. **– COL Tom Snukis, USA(Ret), Associate Professor, Joint and Combined Warfighting School**

In an increasingly complex world, with more and more demands on our time, JC uniquely distills vital, ancient philosophical beliefs as well as practical, active leadership applications from his time as an Army Ranger, and he blends them beautifully to give everyone, regardless of age or profession, a timeless reflection of how to live a life of purpose. **- Christopher B. Angel, Headmaster, Hammond School**

This book's message is good for everyone to read. Human behavior is a huge reason for success and failure in life and this book explains in detail why. **- Jeff Dillman, Director of Football Strength & Conditioning, University of South Carolina**

A must read for those pursuing opportunities to enhance and value the warrior-philosopher within themselves (or their team) and understand what "Lead by example" truly means. No matter if you're a Ranger Squad Leader or a corporate board room member the significance of JCs description on the human minds cycle of greatness and the critical difference between motivation and inspiration is priceless. One of the major challenges within our nation's warrior class is the development of the mind and recognizing a person's threshold of failure while balancing order and chaos during conflict. JC has a lifetime of experience in this arena and best explains how to develop and progress the psychological-warrior mind set with determined thought that is focused on excellence (lethal excellence in most cases) in order to thrive in anarchy. I recommend all to read this book thoroughly and read it often. . . . RLTW! - **CSM(R) Ray A. Devens, JROTC Instructor, Mariner High School Leadership Academy**

"Meditations of an Army Ranger" is a blue print for individual success and self-awareness, using lessons, techniques and experiences that you can apply to your life. The method of expression and explanation of deeper thinking LTC (R) Glick and Dr. Atalanta share, navigates you through a clear understanding of life skills necessary for personal growth and leadership. - **SFC Orlando Soto, The Ohio State University Army ROTC, C CO CEMAT**

The speed of life for a leader can be devastating. Without direction and introspect leaders can be lost in a labyrinth that leads to dead ends and pitfalls. Without discernment and reflection, a leader has no direction, nor the cognitive capacity to grow. One must seek, learn, and reflect to have such growth. This path to growth is forked; a leader can choose personal suffering or learning through the eyes of others. JC's eyes have seen many things and he shares his lessons and experiences in "Meditations of an Army Ranger". This book is a must have book that Generals and CEOs alike should add to their required reading lists. **– Scott Puckett, Veteran Law Enforcement-Protection Professional / Lead Instructor- Sorinex Tactical Applications Group**

As a coach, I understand the necessity of having and implementing a philosophy to inspire a team. JC Glick's [and Alice Atalanta's] "Meditations of an Army Ranger" not only articulates this "warrior philosophy' but establishes a foundational understanding of why it is critical. This book is a truly helpful insight for coaches, teachers, or anyone in leadership. **– Erik Kimrey, Head Coach Football, Hammond School**

Anyone who aspires to living a life of consequence with intention and purpose must anchor themselves in key principles that stand the test of time. The philosophical precepts shared in this book show us the way to living just such a life. A must read for any leader, in any field, with application to any size organization. **– COL John A. O'Grady, U.S. Army, Combat Veteran/Executive Leadership Consultant**

"Meditations of an Army Ranger" by JC and Dr. Atalanta provides invaluable guidance and insights to the development of the transformational leadership philosophy which is extremely applicable in business and in sport. Leaders and those that follow them raise one another to higher levels of morality and motivation and this book is that guide for the process. **- Curt Lamb, Assistant AD for Sports Performance, Limestone College**

Reading Meditation of an Army Ranger is a quick essential way of becoming a self-actualized human being. JC and Alice do a wonderful job relating by example and with the use of analogies what it takes to be successful in these trying times. Their book takes you on a great ride through this Ranger's mind, body and soul. A must read for anyone who wants to achieve success as a leader! **- Francis Savino, Owner and founder of Gridiron Inc. - A Strength and Conditioning facility, Operating since 2003**

Like with his 1st book, J.C. (and Alice) does it again in "Meditations of an Army Ranger" -- making you think and reflect on every page throughout this entire book. They write: "[t]here are no losses: only wins and lessons." This book is not for the warrior, scholar, educator, president(s), executives, or athletes -- it is a must read for all! **- Christopher K. Greca CSM (R), President, 5th Principle LLC**

Also by JC Glick

A Light in the Darkness: Leadership Development for the Unknown, with Sarah Ngu

Arma

(Shield)

She is my Arma

Her love is strong and acts as my protection

Her love is soft and is my comfort

Her love is loyal and emboldens me

Her love is kind and brings me peace

Her love is unwavering and gives me courage

She is my Arma

And

I will never lose her

Hatteras

56 Park Road

Tinton Falls, NJ 07724

www.hatteras.us

Meditations of an Army Ranger: A Warrior Philosophy for Everyone

Opening page poem: JC Glick

Cover design: Joel Carpenter

ISBN 978-0-9988485-1-8

Printed in the United States of America

energy - raw diffuse
effort - focused
directed

MEDITATIONS

OF AN

ARMY RANGER

A WARRIOR PHILOSOPHY FOR EVERYONE

AMAZON BESTSELLING AUTHOR

FORMER ARMY RANGER

J.C. GLICK, LTC, U.S. ARMY, RETIRED

&

DR. ALICE ATALANTA, PH.D.

CONTINENTIAE

PROOEMIUM

(Preface)

MARK DIVINE

EXSUSCITO

(Awaken)

BOOK I: COGITARE ALITER

Thinking Differently

BOOK II: HABERE ET ESSE

(To Have and To Be)

BOOK III: DUCATUS

(Leadership)

BOOK IV: ELECTISSIMI

(Elite)

VADE

(Go Forth)

BIBLIOGRAPHIA

PROOEMIUM

(Preface)

Warriors into the breach!

In this valuable contribution to leadership literature,
Meditations of an Army Ranger, retired Ranger LTC JC
Glick and Dr. Alice Atalanta give us tools and insights to
evolve your personal philosophy and leadership character.
These skills will soon be "The Way" for leaders
attempting to navigate the Volatility, Uncertainty,
Complexity and Ambiguity (VUCA) enveloping the
world. The subtle skills JC and Alice ask us to develop
include virtues such as trustworthiness, vulnerability,
insight, nuance, intuition, and emotional awareness.
Where are those taught today? Even the military
academies, with their exceptional leadership development
programs, do not teach these skills. And yet, they are
crucial.

In my view, the most valuable leadership insights these
days are coming from those who have had to learn these
skills the hard way… in the extreme volatility and
murkiness of combat. Those leaders have dealt with moral
ambiguity and rapidly changing rules of engagement,
often favoring the enemy. Reward came from
accomplishing the mission and coming home to fight
another day. Sometimes, one or more teammates were not
on the return flight. Learning from their losses, these
warriors take nothing for granted, challenge their thinking
on everything, and favor change over the status quo.

Special Operations officers and NCO's are the modern equivalent of ancient Spartans. When warfare dominated the affairs of humans, leaders were warriors, athletes, and philosophers, all in one tightly coiled package. Today, we face the same human condition as the Spartans, but with more sophisticated weaponry. Not surprisingly, Greek Stoicism has found its way into the ranks of the SOF community. But it is not the same form of Stoicism taught by the academics. No, it is something very different.

To the academic, philosophy is all theory and no practice. Stoicism, Existentialism, Platonism and other theories from the distant past are passed about as intellectual candy. But to the warrior leader, philosophy is a life practice, and meaningless unless it works under fire. Special Ops leaders like JC Glick see athleticism as a developmental discipline, leadership as the art of communication, and philosophy as the practice of self-awareness. The bedrock of their philosophy: prepare body, mind, and spirit. Know thyself. Train harder and longer than the enemy. Take care of your teammates. Master the strategy and the tactics. Stay mission focused. Earn trust and respect, every day. Eliminate doubt through action. Get the job done good enough, then rinse and repeat.

Their aim is not glory or gold, but serving their country and teammates, and living meaningful life. Weakness is anathema, but so is self-aggrandizement and puffery. Day in and day out, the warrior leader will ask: "How can I, how can we, be better, do better?"

The most challenging work for this brand of leader is that of self-awareness, where those aforementioned virtues are cultivated. That means forging the mental discipline, concentration and meditation skills to deeply investigate the reality one's own life and see the same truth in others. This is the work of mastery in service to your team and mission.

Like my teammates who have seen the worst, I care deeply about the fate of humanity, or western culture and the Earth. Things appear to be spiraling out of control on multiple fronts. However, I believe we have it inside us to transform into the highest and best version of ourselves, and positively transform humanity in the process. The biggest burden for this change, in my opinion, lies with corporate and non-profit leaders who can have the largest impact on individuals, communities, and the planet. And the philosophy outlined in this book will work for these leaders as effectively as it works for the Army Ranger, the Green Beret, and the Navy SEAL.

Now, corporations permeate virtually every aspect of society, and can facilitate radical positive (think Tesla) or radical negative (think Twitter) change. If you are a leader on the corporate battlefield, then JC, Alice, and I need you to join us in our mission. It will require you to set the example and lead, to develop a new depth of leadership authenticity… mostly through trial and error.

By 2045, my personal mission is to train and inspire 100 million world centric warrior leaders, who will impact a billion, and lead humanity toward more unity and peace. JC and Alice are onboard with this mission, and this book is an important contribution to the cause. Together, as "world centric warrior leaders," we can create a worldwide force for good. When the whole world starts to look like a battlefield, it's time for the warriors to step into the breach. Join us...all hands-on deck.

Hooyah!

Mark Divine
Commander (Ret), US Navy SEALs.
NYT best-selling author The Way of the SEAL and Unbeatable Mind. Founder of SEALFIT, Unbeatable Mind, and Kokoro Yoga

EXSUSCITO

(Awaken)

WHY PHILOSOPHY?

"Learn to ask of all actions,
'Why are they doing that?'
Starting with our own."
· *Marcus Aurelius* ·

"War is the father of all things."
· *Heraclitus* ·

Philosophy is in a predicament: years of being used as a pawn in egocentric battles of intellect by academics has led many regular folks to shun philosophy as if it were nothing more than intellectual wordplay and snobbery. "An indulgence of academics and the unemployed," it is often said. But this is not what western philosophy originated to be.

In an increasingly globalized world of competing belief systems, philosophy can seem like a waste of time to us. We don't place value on contemplation; we are focused on action. Of this mindset, we look for leaders who seem to represent the survival skillset that we think we need.

Seeking after the keys to high performance, we turn our focus to the Special Operations community for guidance. Members of the Special Operations community seem to live their lives like arrows being shot out into the darkness of the unknown: there is no time to ponder; only to act. We think that, if we study and emulate them, we will uncover the keys to becoming our best selves.

In the 1980s, it was Special Forces. In the 90s and 00s, it was the SEALs. We put these teams on a pedestal, because that is what human beings are good at doing. We objectify, worship, and emulate the notion of other human beings whose status we elevate to that of "larger than life." It's a phenomenon that can be observed cross-culturally since the dawn of time. It's not going away. In the United States, we have traditionally reserved this kind of hero worship for movie stars, rock stars, and professional athletes. Now, as the Special Operations community has grown in both visibility and notoriety, we extend it to members of our armed forces.

It is a disconcerting and dangerous phenomenon.

Look around us: we are bombarded by images of these warrior types on every form of media. They are portrayed as strong, fit, square-jawed people of action—not thought. We see them, and we feel compelled to bring some aspect of their identity into our own lives. Buying into the hyper-motivated, superhero-like identity that we are sold, we idolize their example of getting up early to perform over-the-top training regimens, urging ourselves through grueling workouts as we look to emulate what we believe are the secrets to their success. We don our American flag hats and shemaghs in a tribute to them, hoping to touch a piece of what they are all about.

But how well do we truly understand what it takes to be these men and women—and what they truly have to offer beyond the "Special Operations mystique" that we are sold? We look to them to motivate us physically and teach us how to push through challenges, but this is all the leadership and guidance from them that we seek (and, thus, all that we are usually sold). In doing so, we miss the areas where they could be inspiring us as much if not more: in our work and learning pursuits, in the raising of our children, and even in how we look at our relationships, civic duty, and our notions of living a good life.

War, after all, calls upon human capacities above and beyond courage and physical strength. War is perhaps the greatest teacher of human nature; as it affords human beings the opportunity to witness and experience both the highest pinnacles and the deepest nadirs of our existence—often simultaneously. There is violence, hatred, corruption, deception, selfishness, and rage; but there is also discipline, altruism, self-sacrifice, idealism and--above all--love.

But to ask an Army Ranger for advice on raising children? Look to a Green Beret or PJ for insight into the meaning of life? Really?

In a word: maybe. Because our warriors are some of the closest living connections to philosophy that we have.

Whether or not they consider themselves students of philosophy or not, the study of the extremes of human nature is both inherent in and critical to their jobs. We can study books of philosophy in dusty university libraries, and that is one way to come to half of the understanding. But to gain a full understanding—and this is where most academic applications of philosophy fall short—we must look for philosophy paired with practical experience. And there is no better witness to the full gamut of human experience than the warrior. There is a reason why the Meditations of Marcus Aurelius have endured the ages with universal poignancy: he was not just a Stoic philosopher, but also a warrior and emperor. A philosopher with profound personal experience of human life in all its complexity.

To bring philosophy to life requires exposure to the human animal in action. And in war, many of the critical features of our human existence are pushed to the forefront. Soldiers in combat are put into situations that force them to ask themselves questions that are central to philosophy: is God there? Why does God allow war? Are my enemies like me, or are they different? Is it possible to kill but not murder? What is the purpose of my life? Am I a good human being? Is evil real?

War pits our rational selves and capacities against our irrational and animal instincts, which are also called upon in combat. How do we reconcile these things? How do we live with ourselves after we have fought and perhaps killed? How do we address the fact that the ethics that govern our national values on the homeland are by necessity not always the same ethics that can govern our conduct on the battlefield?

These are not small questions. They penetrate deeply into the soul of what it means to be a human being. Philosophers choose to ask them; warriors *have* to ask them.

The authors of this book have both come to this same conclusion, but starting on opposite sides of the coin. One, an academic schooled in philosophy for over a decade, who discovered through the sport of boxing an unexpected resource of insight into human instincts and behavior. The other, a decorated war veteran of over 20 years who, in the aftermath of war, turned like so many others to philosophy for insight into the things he had thought, felt, discovered, and experienced in war.

From ancient times, we have built our human foundations upon the philosophy of warriors. Not on their philosophy of war, but on their philosophy of *life*. How they saw the world. The ideas of democracy, service, education, and love that evolved from earlier generations of human beings who had seen combat. Aside from Christianity, no other moral, ethical, or philosophical system has so greatly impacted Western culture as the teachings of the Ancient Greeks—and not only were the Greeks some of the greatest philosophers the West has ever known; they are also some of the most storied warriors. This is not coincidental. Philosophy, to these ancient warriors, was not a luxury reserved for the privileged, but rather a tool; a necessity required not only to fight better, but to live better.

So much of our world today hinges upon technology, and technology grows in what is mostly a straightforward progression of improvement: first there was radio, then black and white TV, then color, and now we can live stream anything we want on our handheld devices. It is easy to forget that the inner life of human beings does not progress along this same trajectory. We are no wiser today than the Greeks were 2500 years ago. The trajectory of human life is cyclical: we follow cycles and patterns that repeat themselves through time and echo throughout generations. Each human life follows an almost archetypical evolution that resonates repeatedly throughout time and space. The only path to progress is through personal growth founded in the experience of our predecessors.

Contemporary American life is more deeply suffused with the influence of Ancient Greek philosophy than many of us recognize. Our nation's Constitution and Declaration of Independence were created by our founding fathers based on enlightenment principles emphasizing man's natural right to freedom. Underpinning the enlightenment, a European philosophical movement? The works of the Greeks. As English philosopher Alfred North Whitehead once famously stated, "The safest general characterization of the European philosophical tradition is that it consists of a series of footnotes to Plato."[1] In the West, we are all descendants of the Greeks. It is not an exaggeration to say that, as Americans, our entire nation was founded upon a philosophical tradition that originated from a warrior class of philosophers.

---

[1] Alfred North Whitehead, *Process and Reality* (Free Press, 1979).

Bryan Doerries, author of "Theater of War," wrote: "Many of the greatest humanistic achievements of ancient Athens—arguably one of the most militaristic democracies ever to inhabit the earth—were forged in the crucible of constant military conflict. Storytelling, philosophy, art, and war were vitally and inextricably interconnected."[2] Is it thus so surprising that today, as our country is set to complete our second straight decade at war in 2021, that ancient philosophy should be experiencing a resurgence as millions of Americans are now rediscovering ancient thought—particularly that of the Stoics? A war-fatigued nation, grappling with the moral and ethical challenges laid bare before us by a hyper-connected world, we are seeking solace, guidance, and understanding.

The time is now ripe for the return of the warrior-philosopher. We are hungry for it: the wisdom and guidance which can be brought to us by someone with firsthand experience of the real world. What does it really take to lead other human beings? If we are to seek a true substance matter expert on the topic, it behooves us to ask someone who has not only led, but who has led under the most adverse conditions. Only the warrior philosopher can bear witness to the actuality of other humans performing at the apex of their personal capacity while simultaneously witnessing death and downfall in a way that those of us with purely academic expertise can merely conceptualize.

Philosophy on its own can't save us. Left to its own devices, philosophy becomes a self-fueling fire of navel-

---

[2] Brian Doerries, *Theater of War* (Vintage, 2016).

gazing that spirals quickly into the realm of impracticality. The great Stoic philosopher Seneca himself warned of this when he observed, "There are indeed mistakes made, through the fault of our advisors, who teach us how to debate and not how to live. There are also mistakes made by students, who come to their teachers to develop, not their souls, but their wits. Philosophy, the study of wisdom, has become philology, the study of words."[3]

While we need philosophy, as a culture we currently tend to seek motivation from our warriors—and in this, we are missing the mark. Philosophy fills a gap that motivation can't fill. Motivation—whether in the form of a quote, book, meme, song, or social media post—can get us fired up to take the first or the next step towards a goal. On rare occasion, it may get us out of bed for a pre-dawn workout. But motivation has a shelf life; it does nothing when it comes to answering the big questions. It is a cheap (if sometimes necessary) impetus to ask from a sect of society that has so much more perspective to offer us.

All this being said, the book you are holding in your hands is not a work of pure philosophy. It is not designed to pass academic muster or to inspire esoteric debates. The exclusive, erudite, competitive pursuit that philosophy has become, in some academic circles, is not what it originated to be. Philosophy—the marriage of "philo" ("love of") and "sophia" ("wisdom")—is and has only ever been for the sake of one thing: understanding.

---

[3] Lucius Annaeus Seneca, *Letters From a Stoic*, Transl. Robin Campbell (Penguin, 1969).

And to truly understand, we must seek perspective from people who are different from us. In the following pages, you will find exactly that: a glimpse into the lessons learned from one Army Ranger's insights into life and leadership—forged in the crucible of war but elaborated here in a broader context that renders them applicable to all of our lives, regardless of profession.

It is philosophy that serves not to motivate, but to inspire. It is not a philosophy for warriors; it is a philosophy that serves human beings. That's all warriors are, at the end of the day; human beings with a highly specified skillset. But human beings.

It is an examination of how we look at the world, or how we might be able to see the world around us. It is a philosophy that requires us not just to ponder life, but to act on life. To live active lives of *purpose.*

We have called this book "a warrior philosophy for everyone" for a reason. In our contemporary popular imagination, we have become comfortable with a very narrow concept of what it means to be a "warrior." Many embrace what they call the "sheepdog" mentality, emphasizing that warriors are the ones who "run towards the sound of gunfire." In certain circles, the quote oft attributed to George Orwell, that "People sleep peaceably in their beds at night because rough men stand ready to do violence on their behalf," has gained momentum and popularity. This is partially correct: these definitions absolutely do apply in a very literal sense to the members of the military and law enforcement communities who seek to mitigate threats before they touch innocent lives.

But by the same token, we must expand our notion of what it means to be a "warrior" to include all those who run towards the sound of metaphorical "gunfire": those darkest, and perhaps most painful, tender, and intimate corners of human existence from which most of us shield ourselves. Because any time one of us chooses to confront uncomfortable and painful truths, we are acting in the warrior's capacity. Martin Luther King, Jr. Susan B. Anthony. Abraham Lincoln. The Dalai Lama. The hospice caregiver or NICU nurse; volunteers at nonprofit organizations and places of worship working to ease other people's burdens; the child who stands up for another being bullied; the person who gives up more self-serving personal activities to spend quiet time with an aging relative or neighbor. Diverse acts and identities, all, and the possibility for naming them is endless. But the one commonality which they all share is that they involve willfully coming face to face with realities of human existence that are uncomfortable for us to face: aging, illness, mortality, cruelty, poverty, loneliness, inhumanity. Any time we confront these issues head on, we are acting in a warrior's capacity—no different than the Ranger team assaulting the door of a target, charging towards the unknown and the potential for violence and death. At the end of the day, this is what all warriors share: a need to jump into the fray. A need to confront these deepest and most painful issues, and a willingness to accept any risk in the process of doing so—no matter what it may cost us.

We live in a society that privileges us with the possibility of insulating ourselves from many of these concerns, if we wish. We can self-medicate with food, media, and social media, building an inner life of defenses designed to prevent us from facing some of the painful realities of existence. It is easy, possible, and tempting for many to turn a blind eye to matters of great human import. But for those of you who cannot—if you cannot turn your back; if you see suffering and must act; if you cannot live without giving your all to combat suffering, pain, loneliness, and injustice; if you find no thought more noxious than the possibility of living a life without deep purpose—then you, too, are a warrior. And today, perhaps more than ever, our world needs warriors in all aspects of life: government, schools, hospitals, and communities. We need people everywhere identifying the leaky holes and plugging them; running towards the emergencies that they see—both literal and existential—and not being able to live with themselves until they have done all in their power to make a change.

Philosophy is to be the guiding light that illuminates our path when we accept our own warrior's calling. Like Virgil—the great poet of antiquity, who led Dante down through the circles of the Inferno to confront Satan face to face—philosophy is to be our security in these endeavors. It helps to guide our hand and make sense of the nonsensical. It transcends nationality, culture, and faith to touch on universal principles common to all humanity. And it can sustain our sanity in our darkest hour.

When seeking guidance on our own individual warrior paths, we are right to seek motivation from our Special Operations veterans. Still, they are not just sources of information on living lives of action (setting and crushing goals, pushing the limits of our comfort zones and our capabilities). There is an added and critical dimension to this, one that philosophers have pondered since the beginning of time when considering the differences between the active and the contemplative life. The reality is that, as Plato says in the Republic of the scholar-athlete, "He who is only an athlete is too crude, too vulgar, too much a savage. He who is a scholar is too soft, too effeminate. The ideal citizen is the scholar athlete, the man of thought and the man of action."[4] It is, for this reason, our joint effort here to provide a thoughtful leadership philosophy by calling upon both an academic knowledge of philosophical tradition and a practical understanding of human nature—born of wartime leadership experience. Our objective is to provide not just theoretical knowledge, but wisdom—knowledge evolved and tested in the crucible of true human nature.

This is a book for human beings. It contains lessons learned and confirmed through life experiences: giving life, taking life, fighting for one's own life. Philosophy is merely the method of expression and explanation. But the ideas are tools that should carry us forth better armed to face life's challenges than we were before we encountered them. We must temper and guide our impulse to action with contemplation. It is not enough to be people of action. We must strive to be people of thoughtful action— and that is what this book is about.

Whatever each of us seeks from philosophy--whether it is solace and consolation, or advice and guidance--the underpinning is that we are striving to be better. We are fighting against complacency at every turn. We refuse to show up as less than the best possible version of ourselves each and every day. Life is only in part what happens to us. The other part is: what are we going to do about it?

---

[4] Plato, *Republic*, Transl. G.M.A. Grube (Hackett, 1992).

We are not here to merely think;
We are not here to only act;
We are here to think and act.

COGITARE
ALITER
(Thinking Differently)

I. MOTIVATION VS. INSPIRATION

"Don't say you don't have enough time.
You have exactly the same number of hours per day
that were given to Helen Keller, Pasteur,
Michelangelo, Mother Theresa,
Leonardo DaVinci, Thomas Jefferson, and Albert
Einstein."

· *H. Jackson Brown, Jr.* ·

"If you really want to do something, you will work
hard for it."

· *Sir Edmund Hillary* ·

There is an entire industry built around motivation. American culture is hooked on it, and we pour out our hard-earned money for it. We seek motivational speakers, motivational quotes, books, and songs...coaches, psychologists, trainers, and even hypnotists all hawking the same thing. Our hope is that something will click and it will trigger a dormant part of us, and it will move us to unparalleled action. Something inside that will suddenly push us to get out of bed at 5 am to run, journal, do yoga, and meditate. Anything that will strengthen our internal mental resolve to do the things that we know are good for us, because left to our own devices, we lack the resolve to self-motivate.

We believe that motivation works, and so, as leaders, we seek the ability to motivate others. Think about the language that we use when we do so: "I wish I could just light a fire under them," we say. Light a fire *under* them. Motivate them from the outside, like a kettle of water that is waiting to be boiled by an outside stimulus.

But what if the kettle of water could boil itself? What if water could be lit from *within*?

This is the critical difference between motivation and inspiration: motivation comes from an external push—but inspiration comes from inside. Can a motivated person and an inspired person achieve the same thing? Absolutely…but probably not for as long. First, because their processes do not look the same; and second, because the inspired person is fueled by a fire within.

There are two additional differences between motivation and inspiration. First, motivation has a shelf life – it will only last as long as the motivator is forefront in the motivated individual's mind. A social media post from a celebrity athlete first thing in the morning, urging you to get out of bed and hit the gym—it can be motivating, to be sure. But when the stimulus is gone, the motivation can fade just as quickly. The feeling is akin to having a favorite song come on the workout playlist during a run; for those 3.5 minutes, you pick up the pace, only to drop it back down again when the song is over. Motivation can give you a push, in other words, but it doesn't light the fire.

There is another difference. Motivation can be achieved through a negative impetus (es. avoiding pain or punishment). Prisoners in a labor camp may be motivated to work, but the impetus for their labor most certainly does not come from within. Even in a professional or athletic environment, the negative impetus used to motivate is always a possibility. Young recruits in boot camp, for example, are roused from sleep at ungodly hours to run tens of miles under the darkness of night. They are most certainly motivated to do so, and this guarantee comes in the form of the not-so-gentle urgings of their beloved drill sergeant. Like it or not, the recruits are going running.

Perhaps, though, among these young recruits, are a handful of young people with a dream. Individuals who envision themselves completing this training, and then the next and the next until he making their way into a Special Operations unit. Maybe it's been a dream since childhood, inspired by the messages in movies, books, and video games. Whatever the reason, it is their goal, and they own it. Before enlisting, they scoured the internet and talked to a recruiter about it; they know what they are shooting for. And while others may think that they are foolish (the odds are against them making it to the elite level – similar to becoming a professional athlete), they believe in themselves. And so, they haul themselves out of bed, each morning before dawn, to run tens of miles. The drill sergeant is there, but this isn't why they are running. They would be running anyway, because they are inspired. Motivated, for sure, but also inspired. On fire, and chasing a dream.

That's the essential difference between motivation and inspiration. Their end product can be the same—in all cases, the recruits go running—but their processes are not.

Motivation has a starting point and an end point. As long as the drill sergeant is present, come hell or high water those recruits are running. But how many of them would still choose to run on their own if there were nobody overseeing the process? Their reaction is contingent upon an outside stimulus: the drill sergeant.

Aristotle initiated a popular notion of causality that has been influential for thousands of years, and will also be illustrative here. According to Aristotle, everything has four causes: material, formal, efficient, and final. If we were to consider the simple example of a wooden chair, its material cause would be the wood; its formal cause, the idea of what a chair should look like; its final cause, its function to give a human being a place to sit. But its efficient cause is what is of interest to us here: the efficient cause is the immediate action which caused the chair to be—in this case, the actions of the carpenter who crafted it.

Everything in life has an efficient cause; to define it in a single word, an efficient cause is an impetus. And, when it comes to motivation, the efficient cause—the impetus—is external to me. I will get up and run when the Drill Sergeant comes and kicks me out of bed. When it comes to inspiration, however, the efficient cause originates within me: I will get up and run because I choose to; because it matters to ME.

The etymology of the words themselves underlines this difference. "Motivation" takes its root from the Latin *motivus,* for "moving or impelling." Note that to "impel" is to force or urge something into action—just as the drill sergeant dragged the recruits out of bed. "Inspiration" is a far more beautiful concept—it is rooted in the Latin *inspirare*, literally "blow into," but also inspire, excite, or inflame." Inspiration is born of an inner drive. It has been this way for as long as these words themselves have existed, and most definitely longer than that.

Yes, inspiration also allows for an outside impetus. Human beings inspire one another all the time, and inspiration can indeed be born of good leadership. That's what *inspirare* literally means: to breathe into. A good leader can be the one who does the breathing. But just like the goal of rescue breathing in CPR is to get the patient breathing on their own, the leader who inspires will have the same impact on those being led. Like blowing on the tiny ember at the start of a campfire, the goal is always for the fire to catch and to grow on its own. Inspiration works just like that.

If both motivation and inspiration are capable of pushing an individual to action, which one is preferable? It would be better to ask which one withstands adversity better; which is more resilient, and which is more adaptable. The fact is that there is a time limit on motivation: sooner or later, the external stimulus runs out, and the motivation goes away. But inspiration, by nature, has staying power. Look at the world-changing accomplishments of the individuals noted in this chapter's opening quotes: Helen

Keller, Pasteur, Michelangelo, Mother Theresa, Leonardo DaVinci, Albert Einstein, and Sir Edmund Hillary. The endurance required in order reach their humanitarian, political, artistic, athletic, and scientific achievements is testament to the power of inspiration and the resiliency and adaptability that it engenders.

Always keep in mind one thing. Motivation can be achieved by negative means, and its results may not be pretty. The dark side of external motivators is akin to beating a horse to make it run faster, and when human beings have attempted to motivate one another by these types of means, we have arrived at some of the darkest moments in our history. Seek to inspire rather than to motivate; from true inspiration, no wrong can ever come, because inspiration appeals to the best part of our nature. It's what the Greeks called *arete,* the striving for greatness, and it comes from one place only: within.

Amateurs motivate;
Professionals inspire.

II. INTEGRITY VS. HONESTY

*"Every man must decide whether he will walk
in the light of creative altruism,
or in the darkness of destructive selfishness."*

· *Martin Luther King, Jr.* ·

*"All cruel people describe themselves as paragons
of frankness."*

· *Tennessee Williams* ·

*"The whole art of government consists in the art of
being honest."*

· *Thomas Jefferson* ·

The Commander of the Airborne Infantry Brigade brought
the new lieutenants into his office. Pacing authoritatively
through the group, he paused to check each man for a
Ranger tab, speaking pointedly: "Did you go straight
through, or did you recycle? When he came across anyone
who had recycled in Ranger school, earning their tab on
the second try, he wanted to know why. It's not usually a
concern among Rangers who has recycled and who hasn't,
but it felt important to the Commander to ask. Ironically,
the Commander was not a Ranger, himself; he was
Ranger qualified, an honorable but lesser distinction.

Anyone who didn't have the coveted Ranger tab was put on the spot, and an explanation was demanded. Some, embarrassed, admitted they had quit Ranger school. Others had been injured. All kinds of reasons were offered. As junior officers in an Airborne Infantry Brigade tasked with deploying to any contingency within 18 hours of notification, and even though the attrition rate of Ranger School fluctuates between 50-65%, anyone without the tab amongst this cohort understood that they were the exception and not the rule.

The Commander paused before a young man who had an unusual reason for his lack of a Ranger Tab. While he was attending the school, his wife had been diagnosed with cancer; he had elected to drop from the course to be with his wife and support her through her illness and treatment. "How's your wife doing now?" the Commander asked. "She's in full remission, praise God," the Lieutenant's reply.

"I guess you made the wrong choice, then," the Commander said, moving on.

Striding back to the front of the room, the Commander spoke authoritatively, and rattled off a litany of commandments. "Pay all your credit card bills at the end of the month. Do not drive a sports car—driving a sports car tells your Soldiers that you want to drive fast. And, whatever you do," he said, turning address the group, "Do NOT let me catch you with a radar detector. What that tells me is that not only do you want to drive fast; you want to break the law and not pay the consequence."

The Commander had spoken his truth. His version of the truth—the truth as he saw it. The Soldier who had left Ranger school in order to stand by his ailing wife certainly did not share the same version of the truth. Yet, in speaking his version of the truth, the Commander believed that he was doing the right thing, sharing the correct perspective and words of wisdom. He shared his absolute truth. He believed that he was upholding the highest form of integrity by stating his own beliefs as if they were absolute fact, with no regard to the perspective of his audience and their potential objections. In fact, it wasn't that he didn't regard the thoughts of his audience, he not only thought they should be the same (or of course they were wrong), but he didn't care. When he spoke his truth, it wasn't about anyone else; it was only about him. Such is the case when we state our absolute truths.

The Commander, feeling himself to be a man of integrity, stated his sense of the truth: the soldier had made a bad gamble leaving Ranger School, because the wife had survived, and he had missed out on earning his Ranger tab. It was an extraordinarily myopic prioritization of the Commander's belief in the importance of the Ranger tab above all else. Clearly, the Lieutenant did not share this view. But because of the power dynamic their respective offices afforded them, the Lieutenant was not given the opportunity to justify his choice. Additionally, and because we know that his lack of a Ranger tab, rightly or wrongly, had others perceive him as a "less than" leader in this elite unit[5], this sharing of perspective may have led the young leader to believe he was wrong, and doubt his own beliefs.

[Did the feedback help achieve an action or outcome of position of value?]

From a leadership perspective, one must ask: what good did the Commander's "integrity" achieve in this case? Did the Lieutenant learn anything of value? Did the Commander's actions succeed in doing anything more than earning the disgust of the man he was trying to lead?

These nuances—of the presuppositions underpinning what we, as leaders, voice at any given time as "the truth"—matter, especially to our people. For this reason, noted author and educator Barry Jentz has developed a unique model to assist leaders with communication that focuses on developing a perspective of the truth that takes into account our people's needs, perspectives, and points of view. The framework by which he does this sorts our communications at any given time into one of three boxes: The Truth, My Truth, and My Sense of the Truth.

The Truth box is one of absolutes and dichotomies: "yes" and "no," "right" and "wrong," "good" or "bad." There is no discussion or nod to other points of view; there is just one way, and it is the leader's way. The mindset and perspective of this leader is like a fortress, with only one doorway leading out. Nothing else can come in, and whatever is inside the fort is the only thing that exists. There is nothing else.

---

[5] It is important to note that this unit did not require leaders to be Ranger Qualified, unlike Ranger Battalions.

The My Truth box is not quite so absolute, but it is still very clear; answers are still seen in black and white dichotomies. The difference in this case is that the My Truth box is willing to acknowledge the existence of other perspectives—while wholesale dismissing them as wrong. Think of this mindset as a fort with a larger door and other forts around it: it acknowledges that the other forts exist, but it won't take anything new from them, and it won't let anything new inside. Still, this fort will be happy to share whatever it can offer, believing that what it has to give is the best.

The My Sense of the Truth box is the most open perspective. It has ideas of what is right and wrong—good and bad—but it also knows that there is other information out there; additional perspectives that may have the potential to change or modify the original notion. This is a fort with very low walls and doors on every side; it exists surrounded by an infinite number of other forts, trading freely and regularly with all those around it. It knows that its own goods are excellent, but it also acknowledges that there may be even better goods available, and is open to the possibility of trading for them.

What does metaphor look like in practice, when we consider all three senses of the truth at play? Imagine a single event, and then imagine three possible reactions to it. Being cut off while driving in traffic is a common example. The reaction of a driver in the "The Truth" mindset: "What a self-centered idiot! All that person cares about is himself." The "My Truth" perspective: "I don't know what that person was thinking, but what a terrible driver! He might not have seen me, but he is still an idiot for not looking." To respond to this situation with a "My Sense of the Truth" perspective takes a bit more humility and patience: humility to set aside one's own pride and acknowledge another's perspective, and patience to set aside one's own knee-jerk emotional reaction and consider that this might not have been a direct personal attack. The driver in the My Sense of the Truth mindset might respond, "Wow, that was close. I wonder if that person has something on his mind that makes him distracted."

It is natural for most of us to live in the "The Truth" and "My Truth" boxes 95% of the time, but when we are in leadership positions, or when dealing with relationships that are important to us, it is important that we consciously move into the "My Sense of the Truth" space. It is essential if we are to understand the people with whom we are dealing, acknowledging and validating their perspectives.

Years later, after having climbed the ranks to higher offices, that former Commander was dismissed from the Army, ironically due to actions which questioned his own integrity. He had said one thing, but done another, and he paid a heavy price. The significance of this occurrence was not lost on the Lieutenants to whom he had delivered his "radar detector" speech. Nothing erodes respect more quickly than a whiff of hypocrisy. And much of this could have been avoided if he had been able to move into the "My Sense of the Truth" space.

There is a time and a place for integrity, for certain. Consider the words of Frederick Douglass: "I prefer to be true to myself, even at the hazard of incurring the ridicule of others, rather than to be false, and to incur my own abhorrence."[6] But context is important here. Douglass was a former slave turned abolitionist and social reformer. Integrity was critical for him because he carried within himself an experience-based understanding of his truth that needed to be shared with the world. His steadfast belief was critical to his ability to communicate those truths to a world that needed to hear them.

integrity requires context.

Integrity, then, is standing by one's own beliefs at all costs. It is not an inherently bad thing, but it is also not always a good thing, and almost always, it requires context. In the field of leadership, integrity can quickly devolve into a myopic sense of the truth that isolates a leader from the people being led. You see, leaders who verbalize the world as they see it, and then say it is their integrity that has them state their view, implies that their stated view is "right" and all others "wrong". For the leader to equate perspective to integrity is to limit their people and their ideas.

Marcus Aurelius once wrote: "Everything we hear is an opinion, not a fact. Everything we see is a perspective, not the truth." Understanding this relativity, leaders must understand: it behooves us to lead with honesty.

---

[6] Frederick Douglass, *The Essential Frederick Douglass*, Transl. Nicholas Buccola (Hackett, 2016).

The difference between integrity and honesty? Integrity prioritizes your own sense of the truth. Honesty considers the perspective of another. This may seem semantics, and some may argue that they are the same thing. However, "integrity" refers primarily to maintaining a wholeness of self; and thus, when we desire to have integrity, we should consider if the issue we are stating our integrity for is about us alone or about something larger than ourselves. Can I state "my truth" in a way that allows me to be true to myself and not ignore other perspectives? If we think of others first, we tend to identify whether it is an appropriate time to employ integrity.

Conversely, the root of "honesty" is honor: not just of self, but of others. In honesty there is kindness, a share of empathy, and a place of respect for others. Integrity is telling Grandma that her cookies are awful; honesty is finding a more productive truth ("Thank you for taking the time to bake me these cookies"). Honesty speaks to another in a way that integrity never requires itself to consider.

Most of all, honesty is humane. Honesty communicates a leader's Sense of the Truth, perhaps saying something like, "Soldier, your choice to leave Ranger school to be with your wife is not the choice that I would have made, nor is it what I would have counseled you to have done. That being said, I understand why you made that decision, and I respect you. It was a noble sacrifice that you made on her behalf."

Ultimately, which voice would have been more likely to earn this leader his Lieutenant's respect and loyalty? Honesty, while not denying the perspective or authority of the leader, honors the humanity of those who are being led—bringing only positives on both ends of the equation,

honor the humanity of those being led.

Know the difference between the truth, your truth, and your sense of the truth.

III. DISCIPLINE VS. OBEDIENCE

"No person is free who is not master of himself."

• *Epictetus* •

When we imagine the disciplined Soldier, we tend to picture the iconic image of someone impeccably presented in spit-shined boots, high and tight haircut, and perfectly starched uniform. We imagine the self-discipline that it must take to outfit oneself with such meticulous precision, and we project that flawless image onto our perception of the individual. How admirable he or she must be, right? What a perfect Soldier!

But how many people outside of the military feel it's important to spit-shine their own boots before work? The reality is that the "perfect" soldier doesn't shine his boots like that because it actually matters to him, or because it makes him a better warfighter. He shines his boots because he has to. There are repercussions for *not* shining them. Simply put: he gets in trouble if he doesn't shine his boots. That's the only reason he shines them.

And you know what? That's not discipline. That is obedience.

What about the warrior who comes back to the compound after a 24-hour mission, cold, hungry, and tired? Even in his exhaustion, with no one watching, he makes time to complete the important tasks that must be done for him to achieve success on his next mission; and so, he cleans his weapon and his kit, fuels his body with a meal, and goes to sleep to recover his strength. His boots are far from shiny, and as the stubble grows in on his face, he's far from clean-shaven—but what priorities actually impact his effectiveness in battle?

The ones he's looking after. He makes time, while exhausted, to do what needs to be done. Not out of obedience, but out of self-discipline: he understands what needs to be done, and he musters his strength to do the job regardless of how exhausted he is. He is self-motivated to do the right thing, at the right time, for the right reason: the very essence of discipline.

Doing what's right
whether you feel like it or not

We must remember: doing something to avoid consequences is not discipline; it is obedience. Discipline is not acting because we fear a negative consequence; it is acting because we are striving for a desired end.

Dogs should be obedient;
Free men must be disciplined.

IV. EXCUSES VS. REASONS

"Life can only be understood backwards."

• Søren Kierkegaard •

"Any fool can know. The point is to understand."

• Albert Einstein •

"I'm too tired to do this." "I can't go on." "I couldn't possibly finish."

At one time or another, we have all experienced our mind's response to our body's cry to quit. Our body gives us the signal that it's had enough, and the mind dictates the next step. For some people, this means that they quit. Others stop, but follow the dictates of cognitive dissonance and adapt their thinking to convince themselves that they aren't quitters. This is where excuses are formed: "I was up really late last night, so I'm just tired today;" "I'm just not a runner;" "I'll start tomorrow."

We all know that these rationales do no one any good, and excuses have a terrible reputation in the world of sports for precisely this reason. We adopt slogans like "Just Do It" and "No Excuses" to motivate ourselves, and this is a positive: it's never good to accept excuses from yourself. Still, cultivating a no-excuses mindset alone doesn't necessarily mean that one is developing resiliency. These temporary motivational mantras just temporarily silence the inner voice of self-doubt. The inner voice is still there, waiting to appear again and try to drag us down. In other words, the no-fail mantra is not a no-fail solution.

The no-excuses mentality is a catch-22 in the world of Special Operations. On one hand, in order to achieve at the highest level of human performance, it is imperative that operators train their minds to override and ignore their bodies' signals to rest, quit, or give up. Special Operators are not superhuman; they are just human beings who have learned just how much mental control they actually have over their physical bodies. Like any person in the middle of a challenging physical task, their bodies will cry out for rest. However, they cultivate the mental ability to function in spite of these signals, using their minds to push through barriers and achieve an ever-higher level of performance.

On the other hand—and this is the other side of the catch-22—while operators must necessarily cultivate the no-excuses mentality within themselves, when serving in leadership roles, applying this same hard and fast no-excuses mentality when evaluating the performance of others can cause a leader to miss legitimate reasons why things may or may not be working.

When a star player on a team, who is usually a consistent performer, suddenly has a bad game, there is usually a reason. It is not the time or the place to enforce the no-excuses mentality; rather, in this case, the job of the coach—or the leader—is to find out what is going on with this person. In all likelihood, there is an explanation to be found—and hopefully a circumstance to be remedied. Additionally, it is almost too easy (and thoughtless) to provide glib guidance like "no excuses," and to do so puts leaders in danger of not identifying real issues impacting themselves, their people, and their organizations.

In other words, there is a difference between an excuse and a reason, and a thoughtful leader must be able to finesse the difference between the two. Reasons are critical bits of information that need to be assessed, understood, and considered. While in Special Operations Training the no-excuses mentality may help some warriors achieve peak performance, the distinction between reasons and excuses becomes keenly critical when the post-mission After Action Report takes place. If a mission goes well, there are reasons why; if a mission fails, there are reasons why. These reasons, in either case, are not excuses. Many times, when we make excuses, what we are really doing is lying to ourselves or others, whether we believe this to be the case or not. Cognitive dissonance is the culprit here: many times, it is more comfortable for us to invent and believe an excuse we like than to come to terms with a reason that may challenge us, hold us accountable, or make us uncomfortable. Reasons, though not always palatable or easy to accept, are more valuable information in the long term. They express our understanding of a situation, and inform the problem-solving rationale that can lead us to better future outcomes.

In short? A humble leader displays wisdom in respecting the difference between a reason and an excuse, and ensures that they provide better guidance than "no excuses."

The difference between an excuse and a reason is who is giving it, and who is getting it.

V. SITUATIONAL AWARENESS VS. SITUATIONAL UNDERSTANDING

"You get the feeling or the thought first.
How you address this is crucial."
• Tony Blauer •

It's one of the most iconic scenes in movie history: the final 3-way shootout in The Good, The Bad, and The Ugly. Clint Eastwood's character "Blondie" faces off with two other gunslingers for what seems like an eternity; the camera cutting back and forth between the three men repeatedly, its angles increasingly tightening onto the men's gazes as the moment of truth nears. Blondie fires; one enemy drops, and the other man's revolver clicks, having already been surreptitiously unloaded by the scene's hero. Blondie stands victorious, ready to fight another day.

Two thousand years ago, Roman poet Horace wrote that the aim of art is to "delight and instruct."[7] And, indeed, the excitement of this scene titillates our senses—that is the delight part—but it also does something more: it instructs. Through this scene, we are introduced to a

---

[7] Horace, "Ars Poetica," In *The Norton Anthology of Theory and Criticism.* Ed. Vincent B. Leitch (Norton: 2001).

critically important principle: the difference between situational awareness and situational understanding.

"Situational awareness" has become a military buzzword in recent years, and has it has since made its way into popular culture. One is now as likely to hear it on the football field or at the police academy as on the battlefield. As the reputation of Special Operations has gained clout in the public imagination, this term has become one of the features of Special Operations parlance that has been adopted by coaches and leaders who want their people to perform at an elite level. The only problem? They often employ this term improperly—and it begs for clarification.

Consider the scene again. All three gunslingers in this classic western demonstrate situational awareness. They know what is going on around them. They know everyone's position; they see every movement; and they are cognizant of what is in front of them, next to them, and behind them—in short, they are aware. It's a simple scenario: three men, squaring off, pistols pointed at one another. Situational awareness reveals this, and each of them clearly comprehends these basics.

But situational awareness alone only explains half of the scene; someone who has seen more than a fair share of gunfights will pick up on additional details. What information the camera gives us is the same amount of visual data that our situational awareness will detect. But there is a "so what" to every single detail of the scene—reasons that give meaning to everything that we are shown. Blondie's eyes, as they move between the telling details that he observes, guide our understanding to follow his own. He watches the shift of a hand—that's his situational awareness—and his understanding develops that thought: where is the hand going? Closer to the gun—which means a faster draw—or farther from the gun, which could buy him precious milliseconds? Shifts of the feet, sidelong glances, opportunities to take cover—the camera finds each through Blondie's eyes.

In each of these mental computations, Blondie is picking up on subtleties and pre-contact cues that anticipate different potential outcomes of the gunfight. To shoot left or right? Who will draw first? Ultimately, the viewer learns, Blondie had previously unloaded one of the other men's guns in anticipation of the shootout. It catches everyone else off guard; no one else had thought that far ahead—but Blondie did, and his superior level of situational understanding is why he prevailed.

The lesson?

It is not enough to merely know what is going on around you (situational awareness). You need to know what it means—the "so what" of everything you see. And *that* is situational understanding.

In the Special Operations world, no strategy is devised until situational understanding is achieved. Suppose there is a house which is known to be frequented by a specific high value target. The path towards situational understanding begins with pure data: signals indicating the comings and goings of different individuals, for example. This data is the product of situational awareness. With some basic analysis, this data becomes information which tells a story: based on the signals, the target appears to be home in the morning and overnight; there are children on the premises in the afternoon and at night; there are usually 4 bodyguards present, and only 3 bodyguards on Tuesdays. It is this information, coupled with the operators' imperative to capture or kill the high value target, that fuels the situational understanding needed in order for them to plan a mission.

Their mission, based on situational understanding, may look like this: there is a window of time to strike on a Tuesday morning, when children will not be present and there will likely be only 3 bodyguards. Of course, this plan will have branches and sequels. What if the fourth bodyguard turns out to be there? What if a child is in the home? There are plans and strategies put in place for each foreseen contingency.

Situational understanding, in other words, is the precursor to strategy. Any strategy that is not founded upon situational understanding is mere conjecture. To put it simply, situational understanding takes situational awareness and asks: "So what?"

Just remember this principle: whether in a gunfight, the workplace, or on the athletic field, situational awareness alone is only the observance of details; situational understanding is how details translate to action. I see what is happening—so what do I need to do next? It is this level of understanding—and knowing the answer to "So what?"—that will make you quickest to the draw.

Knowing what is going on around you is good;
Knowing what it means is better.

VI. SUCCESS VS. ACHIEVEMENT

"What is defeat?
Nothing but education.
Nothing but the first step to something better."
· Wendell Phillips ·

Fame. Fortune. Celebrity. Status.

Some may call them national obsessions; others may feel
that, in the age of digital media, the relentless pursuit of
all of the above has become globally commonplace.
Human beings have always competed for status, after all.
Every society known to humankind has displayed
evidence of this. For better or for worse, seeking status is
a foundational characteristic of who and what we are.

Of course, for measures of status to be defined, human
beings have historically named them. Degrees, offices,
and awards; from the Boy and Girl Scouts to the Ivy
League to the Army, we assign titles to these things. We
symbolize them, pin them to our chests, or draw up formal
looking degrees to frame for the wall of the office. These
are all markers of our achievements, and we use them to
define and rank ourselves—and one another.

This is all well and good. Surely, we all glean critical
information from achievements and credentials, and it's

often necessary to know what they are. After all, an M.B.A. may make a wonderful executive, but we wouldn't ask a businessperson to perform our heart transplant. And many achievements are the product of accomplishments which are, indeed, worthy of respect.

The problem arises when we look at others and conflate their achievements with success, thereby undermining our own self-worth—and our valuation of others—based on the achievements we perceive ourselves to be lacking. When tempted to do this, we must pause and ask ourselves—do achievements always necessarily indicate success?

Some achievements come easily, after all. A politician who runs uncontested for office will inevitably achieve their goal. A fighter can walk through a tournament without an opponent in their weight division and win a title without throwing a single punch. But what lesson is learned when an achievement is made in the absence of striving? Are we truly any better for it? Any wiser? Stronger?

The truth of the matter—to which anyone who has ever aimed high and missed the mark can attest—is that true success comes in the form of the lessons we learn from the hard work and striving, whether we reach our intended outcome or fail. Achievements may be indicators of victory, but they may also arrive hollow when we do not have to work hard for them. Success, however, is never hollow. It is the fulfilling and deeply gratifying reward of a job well done. A best effort given. Of performing at the peak of our capability, even when it is not enough to earn us a victory.

Many in the U.S. military today refer to this process as "embracing the suck." To the Stoics, it was the notion of *amor fati*: love your fate. Regardless of space, time, and lexicon, the notion remains the same: no matter what is happening to you, embrace the present moment and appreciate its role in your personal evolution into a stronger, better person. It may be the easy times that we enjoy, but it is through the hard times that we grow.

After the struggle or best effort is complete, achievements may or may not follow. We may summit Everest, or a storm may roll in on summit day. The storm may impede our ability to achieve the title of "one who has summited Everest," but it is entirely out of our control. The best effort that carried us, step after step, to the highest camp on the mountain—within striking distance of the summit—is not. And we must understand the value of that successful attempt. If we miss that brief moment of enjoying the summit's vistas, do we really benefit any less from the lessons that we learned along the journey, and the weeks of climbing and acclimation leading up to summit day? Summit or not, the same lessons learned along the way are most deeply ingrained upon us. As long as we are learning, we are successful—no matter what we ultimately achieve. *positive behavior transformed change/indicates learning skill*

It is important not to confuse this concept with complacency, because there is a huge difference in loving (or even just accepting) your fate and being complacent. Complacency is getting to a certain point in your journey—whether through success or failure—and then determining that nothing more can be done to change your station. It is allowing yourself to believe that there is no action you can take to move forward and do something else, whether it be achieving a greater goal, or just exiting an undesirable situation. Accepting your fate and embracing the suck is about welcoming where you are at that moment and allowing it to teach you something, but also about simultaneously formulating a plan to move on and move forward in order to change your current position. Complacency is stagnant; *amor fati*—loving one's fate—is active.

Marcus Aurelius wrote: "Love nothing but that which comes to you woven in the pattern of your destiny." While we may reach for great achievements, it is critical to accept that sometimes those achievements are not a part of our destiny. It is in striving for them, though, that our deepest learning is done. This is what we must never forget.

Don't confuse success and achievement;
You can get one without the other,
But enough of one will definitely get the other.

VII. SOCIAL CONTRACT VS. PERSONAL RESPONSIBILITY

"What a man loses by the social contract is his natural liberty

and an unlimited right to everything he tries to get and succeeds in getting;

what he gains is civil liberty and the proprietorship of all he possesses."

·*Jean-Jacques Rousseau*·

"The only thing necessary for the triumph of evil

is for good men to do nothing."

·*Edmund Burke*·

One of the principal founding theories of the American system of governance is that of the social contract. It is the institutionalization of the golden rule; assurance that, as we do unto others as we would have done unto ourselves, our fellow Americans are legally bound to do the same. Our founding fathers understood that we would give up some individual freedoms in order to ensure political liberty and civil rights for all, but the individual protections and rights we all obtain as we abide by the social contract make these small sacrifices worth the trade.

When implemented as it is theorized, the system works beautifully. Abiding by the social contract means respecting one another's right to life, liberty, pursuit of happiness—as well as integrity of body and property. As we do so, we should ideally feel encouraged that our countrymen and women would do the same. Of course, in reality, this is a utopian vision, one into which entropy is easily introduced the moment an individual chooses to deviate and—unchecked—disregard the social contract.

And so, we have thieves, criminals, rapists, vandals...the list of social deviances is nearly infinite. But the underlying principal of social deviance is universal. It is, by definition, wanton disregard for what is legal, moral, and/or ethical. Deviance from the social contract.

When explained in these terms, the social contract is simple to comprehend. When it is broken, the burden of responsibility is placed squarely upon the shoulders of the individual who chooses to break it. It should be very clear.

But we don't tend to see it this way, instead often taking personal responsibility for another person's choices. An illustration: you leave your wallet on the front seat of the car, which is locked and parked in your driveway. The next morning, you find your window smashed and your wallet missing. You kick yourself for having left your wallet in full view. Was the theft of your wallet actually your fault? Yes, it was low hanging fruit, ripe to be plucked by the first immoral passerby. Still, is the thief's choice to damage and steal your property something for which you should take responsibility?

Another, far more painful but frequently witnessed example is that of the victim of violent crime whose character is put on trial alongside that of their assailant. If you are mugged walking home alone down a dark street at night, is it your fault for making yourself vulnerable to such an attack?

Many would say that it is. But there is a subtle—yet critical—distinction to be made, and it is one regarding the assignment of responsibility. Anyone who has been the casualty of an unfortunate event can look back and identify things that they might have done differently to have prevented the event's occurrence. You could have brought your wallet inside. You might have called a cab instead of choosing to walk.

BUT.

All of these things can still be true, and yet—here is the critical distinction—the criminal must not be absolved of responsibility. Yes, any of the individuals in the above scenarios might have made a different choice. But the choice to walk home alone is not an inherently dangerous one—at least, it shouldn't be – and it is certainly not against our social contract. These are things that free people in a free country should be able to do; these are the freedoms that our social contract is trying to ensure. If we assign personal responsibility to the casualties in these situations, we are saying that the social contract doesn't matter, when it's the thing that should matter the most.

This, of course, is an aspirational goal. We will not always be moral, honest, upright and trustworthy citizens. We will make mistakes—sometimes by incontinence, and sometimes by intent. We will wrong one another in the course of our lives, and break social contract. In those moments, however, we need to immediately own our actions and accept accountability, never blaming those we have wronged or arguing that we were somehow compelled by outside circumstances to do so.

We must all do our best to be champions of the social contract by being strong, moral, honest, upright, and trustworthy citizens and community members—and raising our children to do the same. If we allow our mindset to shift towards one of taking personal responsibility for others' wrongdoing, we go down a slippery slope towards delegitimizing the social contract. It is something we cannot afford to do if we wish to honor the dream of freedom and equality upon which our nation was founded. Instead, we must manifest appropriate outrage towards those who would choose to break or undermine it.

Accountability must be on those who violate social contract.

VIII. TRANSACTIONAL RELATIONSHIPS

VS.

TRANSFORMATIONAL RELATIONSHIPS

"Those who are happiest are those who do the most for others."

· *Booker T. Washington* ·

"A bone to the dog is not charity.
Charity is the bone shared with the dog,
When you are just as hungry as the dog."

· *Jack London* ·

Altruism. Charity. *Agape. Caritas. Maitrī.* Loving-kindness.

Regardless of the source of the literary, philosophical, or spiritual tradition, the concept of selfless human love is highly valued across cultures. Though it is believed by some who cite evidence from the animal world that altruism is not a uniquely human characteristic, human beings certainly display a unique understanding of altruism as a desirable behavior that must be cultivated and prioritized. In other words, we know that it's a good thing to be selfless—but we also acknowledge that we require reminding from time to time.

Our unfortunate tendency is to see our relationships as transactional; the *quid pro quo* type that says, "I'll scratch your back if you scratch mine." This comes as instinctively to us as trade or barter; even young children understand that transactional relationships work well because they are mutually beneficial.

When love matures to altruism, however, our relationships likewise mature from transactional to transformational. We have reached this point when we recognize that what we get out of a relationship is not what another person gives us, but rather what we ourselves put into it.

The math of this reasoning seems irrational. How can you "get out what you put in?" But human relationships and the workings of the heart and conscience are far too complex to be subject to the reductive simplicity of economics. Martin Luther King, Jr. wrote, in his Letter from Birmingham Jail:

> *"In a real sense all life is inter-related. All men are caught in an inescapable network of mutuality, tied in a single garment of destiny. Whatever affects one directly, affects all indirectly. I can never be what I ought to be until you are what you ought to be, and you*

can never be what you ought to be until I am what I ought to be. "[8]

In other words, our ability to survive as individuals and as a species will always rely upon our ability to take care of one another. When serving others, we do more than help them out. We heal ourselves through the process.

Members of the military and law enforcement communities are frequently trained in the process of "elicitation," or gathering information from a complete stranger. This often begins with ingratiating a formerly unknown and likely untrusting individual. One of the quickest ways to do this? It isn't as they show in the movies, where the detective walks in and offers up a piece of gum or a smoke. In fact—surprisingly—these things have been shown to damage trust, and can raise suspicions on the part of the interviewee. It is actually far more effective to create the circumstances such that the individual waiting to be questioned is able to do a small kindness for the interrogator—share a pen, for example. What again seems counterintuitive is proven by studies in human psychology: we like people when we feel like we have helped them.

Helping you makes me feel good about me.

---

[8] Martin Luther King, Jr., *A Testament of Hope: The Essential Writings and Speeches*, Ed. James M. Washington (HarperOne: 2003).

The important lesson is that, in a world where transactional relationships are the norm, we—as leaders—need to identify every opportunity we can to be transformational. Transforming others' lives, transforming our environment, transforming the world around us…by doing good for others, we ourselves will reap the rewards. Not in a transactional way that lines our pockets or fills our bank accounts, but rather in a human way, that fills our souls and our spirits.

By doing good for others, we ourselves will reap the rewards;
Not transactionally filling our pockets and bank accounts,
But in a human way, filling our souls and spirits.

IX. HARD WORK VS. SMART WORK

"If I had six hours to chop down a tree,
I'd spend the first four hours sharpening the axe."
·Abraham Lincoln·

"Practice does not make the athlete.
It is the quality and intensity of practice that makes the athlete,
not just repeated practicing."
·Ray Meyer·

Special Operations warriors have always been known as "hard workers." They relish not only that title, but the hard work itself. The pride of accomplishing a difficult task—of feeling the sweat through your uniform and the pain that goes to your bones—there is an indescribable feeling of elation in knowing that you accomplished something others would or could not. But what most people don't know is that what actually makes Special Operators special is that they work as smart as they work hard. There is a simple economy to this: the smarter one always works, they believe, the better—because one never knows when they will be left with no choice but to have to work harder.

Learning to prioritize smart work over hard work once saved one of America's greatest pastimes. Football, as we know it, almost didn't exist. In 1905, after a number of students died from injuries suffered in football games, parents in Illinois and Wisconsin began lobbying to have the sport outlawed. It was simply far too brutal. President Roosevelt, in an attempt to save the game and address that year's record 19 football deaths, reached out to Harvard president Charles Eliot in hopes that the game could be made safer instead of outright banned. The adaptations which resulted from this initial contact resulted in the game that we know and love today. Instead of the brutal free-for-all which football first was at its inception, adjustments such as the forward pass and ten-yard first down, as well as the establishment of a precursor to the NCAA, saved the sport.[9]

A century later, boxing and mixed martial arts are undergoing similar transformations. Sports once celebrated for their raw brutality are now being rethought—at the very least on the training level. Now that a significant body of research exists on the negative outcomes from repeated head trauma and concussions, athletes and their coaches have become more accepting of ways to minimize the amount of trauma that they sustain. The old school mindset of fighters who sought to slug it out with round after round of hard sparring—going 100%, 100% of the time—are now being replaced by a younger

---

[9] Whet Moser, "A Brief History of Football Head Injuries and a Look Towards the Future," ChicagoMag.com. 5/4/12. Accessed 12/3/18. http://www.chicagomag.com/Chicago-Magazine/The-312/May-2012/A-Brief-History-of-Football-Head-Injuries-and-a-Look-Towards-the-Future/.

generation of fighters like legendary MMA athlete Donald "Cowboy" Cerrone, who has achieved the shared distinction of most wins in UFC history while having chosen to eschew sparring altogether. "Sparring is all I did; that's what I used to do," Cerrone reflected when he revealed the change in his training; "I thought that I was getting ready for a fight, so I would just be f***ing throwing down. Now, I don't spar at all. All I do is drill, because drilling is the most important thing you can do."[10]

What both of these adaptations are about is simple: hard work versus smart work. The common mentality that many of us share, especially in older generations, is that the harder you work, the better. The cultural clichés surrounding the notion of hard work abound; one thinks of the popular quote "I am a great believer in luck; the harder I work, the more I have of it," which frequently circulates online; though oft erroneously attributed to Thomas Jefferson, can in fact be traced back to a 16th Century English proverb, "Diligence is the mother of good luck." Regardless of the source, the message remains the same: when it comes to hard work, more is always more.

But is it really? As the example of the game of football at its inception demonstrates, preaching only the gospel of hard work sometimes prohibits the innovations and adaptations that smart work can enable. That's all

---

[10] Jenness, Kirik. "Cowboy Removed Hard Sparring From Training." Mixedmartialarts.com. 8/31/16. Accessed 12/3/18.
https://www.mixedmartialarts.com/news/cowboy-removed-hard-sparring-from-training.

"working smarter" really means, after all. Hard work and smart work need not be mutually exclusive. But "working smart" means that we are not too proud to pause and ask if there is an easier or better way to do something. Smart work is questioning the way that things have always been done, and asking if they may be done better. Can risks or waste be further minimized? Can efficiency be increased?

Working smarter asks, "How can we make the game of football safer without banning it altogether?" It considers, "Can I rethink my sparring practices and preserve my brain health while still training to win fights?" Smart work also asks, "Is this business procedure really the best way to get the job done, or is it just the way that we have always done it?" Smart work, above all, is comfortable moving outside the comfort zone of "the way things have always been done." Instead, it refuses to accept that as a viable answer. The answer given by smart work is always, "How can we do this better?" Smart work prioritizes efficiency and the preservation of resources while maintaining or increasing positive outcomes.

The only true obstacle to working smarter is our pride. We must free ourselves from the presupposition that "the way things have always been done" is necessarily the best way, and have the courage to question the status quo. How many great innovations upon which we have come to rely were born of the desire to work smarter instead of harder?

Hard work for hard work's sake is just...hard.

X. CHANGE VS. EVOLUTION

"Taking a new step, uttering a new word, is what people fear most."

·*Fyodor Dostoyevsky*·

"Whilst this planet has gone cycling on according to the fixed law of gravity,

from so simple a beginning endless forms most beautiful and wonderful

have been, and are being, evolved."

·*Charles Darwin*·

New leaders are often faced with a predicament as soon as they step into a new leadership position. In one way or another, they've assumed this role because change is needed, wanted, or warranted. Still, just because change is in order does not mean that it will be welcomed. Change, after all, is a curious thing.

Some of us crave it, seeking after it with insatiable thirst. The individuals who live like this, on the cusp of their comfort zone, understand that they must constantly stretch the boundary of the familiar in order to grow. True growth, after all, never occurs within the realm of familiar. How could it? How could we develop new skills within the circle of that which we've already mastered? So those who pursue greatness constantly push and stretch that boundary. They seek the edge of what they know and purposely thrust themselves into the realm of the unfamiliar, forcing themselves to sink or swim and develop precious new skills, understanding, and capabilities along the way.

Most people who live like this are already leaders. This is the mindset that you find among high performers in any field—the one constant, from CEOs to CrossFit champions, is that these are individuals who have learned to seek the unknown in order to grow. While it is surely a recipe for greatness, it is not, however, the norm. And while high performing leaders may be tempted to see other people's more average within-the-comfort-zone baseline as complacency or stagnancy, a slightly gentler judgement may be in order. We are all creatures of comfort, and many people embrace that. Habitual behaviors within the realm of the familiar are a sure bet for survival, after all; most living creatures tend to find what works and pursue that for the duration of their lives.

The trick, then, is for leaders—who embrace the more hard-charging mindset of seeking change, growth, and excellence—to help nudge their teams out of the comfort zone of the familiar. This must occur for an organization to grow, but how is it to be done when in most people's minds, familiarity means safety—and safety is good?

The answer is simple: redefine change. What are you really asking your team to do, after all, when you ask them to break out of the familiar mold and embrace new practices and perspectives? You're not asking them to leave behind all of the good things that they were already doing right. You're just asking them to grow and build on those things.

You're asking them to evolve.

Redefine change as evolution in your own mind and in the terms with which you address the subject with your people. The notion of evolution is a universal positive: it implies growth based on the improvement of our strengths. Just as in the scientific theory of evolution a creature's non-adaptable features become vestigial and are eventually lost, so in the broader notion of evolution, habits and beliefs that are no longer adaptable may be left behind in favor of more advantageous practices.

If your people are resistant to change, try employing this analogy from the world of Special Operations. In SEAL training, when various exercises are performed throughout the course of a day, they are referred to as "evolutions." So, the day's first evolution may be a two-mile ocean swim, followed by a beach run in boots for time/distance, and so-forth. Why use the term "evolution" instead of "exercise" or "activity?" Think about the purpose of the activities. The idea is not that the men perform the exercise perfectly for the first time on day one and then perfectly every subsequent time for the duration of their months of training. Rather, the objective is that the men improve with each subsequent evolution, so that when they earn the coveted Trident, they are better and stronger than they were when they started. Not changed…but evolved.

As leaders, we must ask our people to grow; not change. Change implies that something was wrong with who they were. Evolution means that they can be a better version of themselves. As such, let us look to evolve our people and our organizations—building upon great foundations to build something better than we ever may have first imagined.

No one likes to change, but everyone wants to evolve.

XI. COMMITMENT VS. PASSION

"Desire is the key to motivation, but it's determination and commitment to an unrelenting pursuit of your goal—a commitment to excellence—that will enable you to attain the success you seek."
· *Mario Andretti* ·

"Most people fail, not because of lack of desire, but because of lack of commitment."
· *Vince Lombardi, Jr.* ·

In the early stages of love, our brains are flooded with a delicious cocktail of chemicals that intoxicate us with a near obsession for our partner. Grand gestures, great works of art, music, and literature, heroic acts, even wars fought and won (the woman's face who sailed 1,000 ships): there is no denying that human beings in the throes of passion are capable of great things.

But feelings of passion can inspire some not-so-great things, as well. Van Gogh's ear. The archetypical "crime of passion." Modern day political protests which turn to violence in the streets. Fist fights and shoving matches on the athletic field. Passion run amok can be dangerous, wild, and damaging.

This happens because passion, at its core as an emotion, is by definition irrational. No amount of rationalizing in a therapist's chair can rekindle the spark of irrational, wild passion that once burned in a marriage gone cold. Wishing for the passion to return can't bring it back, nor can seeking to understand or explain it; passion is, by nature, elusive in that way. It doesn't play nice or come when it's called.

For this reason, when we are talking about teams, passion cannot be trusted. Passion waxes and wanes, and that is not a risk that a high performing team can afford to take. There needs to be more on the table to ensure that efforts will continue even when passion has waned—and that's where commitment comes in.

For example, in any relationship, commitment is the glue that holds a couple together once the early-on intoxication of interest, or even passion, subside. True commitment to others is characterized by a promise that our efforts—at anything—will persist.

As leaders, we tend to say that we want our people to be passionate about what they do. But do we? Do we want our people to be passionate, or do we want them to be committed?

The beauty of commitment is its promise to endure—*no matter what.* Passion can't promise that. In fact, passion in the workplace or the athletic field can be a detriment to performance, because it can impede objectivity and collaboration among individuals whose passions may not coincide.

As athletes, Soldiers, executives, or parents, what keeps us pushing forward on the days when everything feels like it's falling apart? When our bodies ache, when we are slammed by tragedy, or when circumstances feel insurmountable? In the Special Operations world, Survival, Evasion, Resistance and Escape (SERE) training is implemented to drive home this very point. When one is in a simulated POW environment, all passion and enthusiasm are quickly burned through until nothing is left but commitment. Personal motives for commitment may vary—getting home to one's family, completing training, earning a coveted spot on a SOF team, not letting down teammates—but for all who graduate from SERE school, the one constant behind their success is the degree of their commitment to achieving their desired end state.

Commitment is getting up every morning at 4 am to run, meditate, and eat properly before work. Commitment is staying up all night with a sick child or aging parent, even when you are sick yourself. Commitment is passing the ball off to a teammate and letting them score the winning goal, giving up your shot at personal glory for a better bet that's more likely to bring home the W for the team. Commitment is putting in the work even when you don't feel like it, and commitment is self-sacrificing. But when everyone on a team shares the same degree of commitment, that slack will get picked up—like the hoplite shield which was held by one man but which protected both brothers beside him.

As with many things, commitment can certainly be broken. We see this in failed marriages, lost friendships, and careers left behind. However, the difference between lost passion and broken commitment is choice. When passion is lost, it is an uncontrolled emotion that is gone; not because we decide to give it up, but because our heart does. When we break a commitment, however, we make a choice: a deliberate and conscious decision not to continue that to which we had previously committed ourselves. And in that distinction, we see that we hold no power over passion, but we have complete control of our commitment.

For these reasons, always look for committed people over passionate ones. Commitment will endure far longer than passion ever could.

Passion does not sustain our forward movement;
commitment does.
With passion, commitment can ebb and flow;
With commitment alone, we are steady in our effort.

XII. FAIR VS. EQUAL

"Fairness does not mean everyone gets the same.
Fairness means everyone gets what they need."
・*Rick Riordan*・

"I have always found that mercy bears richer fruits
than strict justice."
・*Abraham Lincoln*・

Parents or not, we have all been children once. And, if we plumb the depths of our memories, we can think back and remember how much the concept of "fairness" mattered to us in childhood. We would watch our siblings like little hawks, keeping tabs of who got the slightly bigger scoop of ice cream; taking turns was paramount; a game of "eeny meeny miny moe" or drawing straws made seemingly impossible choices for us. We would howl the tiresome words that every parent of school-aged children comes, at some point, to dread: "It's not FAIR!"

But a child's concept of fairness is limited by their developmental stage and intellectual capacity. When a child asks adults to be fair, what they are really requesting is that the adults be equitable. If we have one donut, we split it 50/50. That is perfectly equitable, and it makes sense to a child. If my sibling gets to choose the first TV show we watch, I get to choose the second, and so forth. Equality is easy to discern: it is simply based upon a comparative analysis of two things. When children ask for "fairness," what they are really requesting is equality. A simple proportional split among all invested parties, however best that may be achieved.

True fairness is far more complex. Fairness is not only based upon quantitative measures; it takes into account additional considerations. Fairness is not just that each party gets an equal piece of the pie; it is that they get a proportional piece of the pie that makes sense, all things considered. Fairness says that dad gets a bigger helping of ice cream than a 2-year-old, because dad is much bigger. It's not an equitable division of ice cream, but it's a fair split: each one gets as much ice cream as their body can actually handle.

A better example, again borrowed from the family context, is that of two siblings outside practicing archery. There is only one bow and one target, so the children are going to have to take turns. The older child goes first, and places three shots on target; it comes easily. When the younger child takes a turn, parental help is needed, and it takes this child longer. It would be equitable to say that each child gets a timed turn of equal length. But is this really fair? The younger child, still learning, takes longer to get off one shot, and requires more assistance—this child will arguably benefit less per minute of practice than the older child will. Will the equitable solution really work well to meet the needs of both?

In a scenario like this, the fair solution is a better answer. The fair solution may be to give each child a chance to take a set number of shots on target. Whether one child takes longer than the other is immaterial; both will get the practice and coaching that they need. All things considered, at the end of the day, it will not have been an equitable division of time—but their mutual experience in practicing archery will have been fair, all things considered.

Equality is easy; it is thoughtless. But fairness requires empathy. It requires consideration.

Unfortunately, the law has difficulty being fair. It would be impossible to write laws that account for every possible contingency which could impact fair outcomes. As such, we often define justice in terms of equality, and measure equality against set standards. But equality, in these terms, doesn't always consider all factors. When two people arrive in traffic court for speeding 60 through a 25-mph zone, both will face the equal brunt of the law. Still, holding them to this same standard may ignore critical mitigating details: perhaps one driver was drag racing, while the other was rushing his pregnant wife to the hospital; maybe one has received ten tickets for speeding violations in the past year, while the other has never received a ticket in their lives. These contingencies most certainly matter, and they merit consideration.

As adult leaders, achieving fairness will never be easy. An equitable solution can be enforced uncontested; it is easier for us as leaders. But it is critical to recognize that fairness *feels* better to our people, and as such, we should seek to achieve it wherever and whenever possible.

As leaders, we will always have an opportunity to be equal or fair—in the eyes of our people, and in our own hearts. Remember that equality is easy, and that fairness requires thought. Do what is right for your people, your organization, and for you—in that order.

Fair is not always equal, and equal is almost never fair.

XIII. ACCOUNTABILITY VS. RESPONSIBILITY

"The greatest leader is not necessarily the one who does the greatest things.

He is the one that gets the people to do the greatest things."

• *Ronald Reagan* •

"Never tell people how to do things. Tell them what to do, and they will surprise you with their ingenuity."

• *General George Patton* •

Accountability and responsibility. As leaders, we frequently talk about these as if they were the same thing—but in doing so, we miss a critical conceptual difference: that of ownership.

When a leader devises a plan, and provides their people with detailed instructions on how the plan should be implemented, it is the leader who is ultimately accountable for the plan. Yes, each individual is responsible for completing his or her assignment, but the plan's ultimate success or failure falls on the leader's shoulders. The leader owns that plan.

Conversely, when a leader comes to the team and says, "This is what needs to happen," the onus is on the team to devise a viable solution. If the solution succeeds or fails, the team who devised the solution is accountable for the outcome. In this scenario, it is the team who owns the plan.

In a military context, where decisions impacting life and death hang in the balance, these are critical distinctions to be made. When soldiers are given orders, the carrying out of those orders is their individual responsibility. However, should those orders turn out to have been the wrong tactical decision, accountability lies on the shoulders of the leadership who devised them. The leader is the one who must own the decision.

In the civilian world, this boils down less to finding the accountable party for team successes and failures, and more about the style of leadership that is best for our people. When individuals are given the freedom to devise solutions, they take ownership for their actions—and this sense of ownership naturally gives rise to the accountability that leaders so frequently report that they would wish to see more of in their teams. As leaders, we cannot expect our teams to be accountable for their actions if they are only taking orders from us. We have to let people problem solve, and create an environment that is less draconian where they act only when ordered to do so. Under this dynamic, leaders become more like instructors, helping teams along to find success on their own.

For some leaders, it is a struggle to renounce this much control. What if our people fail? And the simple answer is that if they do, that's why the leader is there. The leader's job is to act as a catalyst, eliciting the highest performance from the team and keeping each member operating at their maximum potential. The leader is there to guide them, and to make tough calls when there is no consensus. But people who are given flexibility and opportunity for free thinking and innovation by their leaders are not just more productive and empowered; they are the people who end up being accountable for their actions—just as we say we want them to be.

To get accountability, you have to give ownership.

XIV. SYMPATHY VS. EMPATHY

*"Resolve to be tender with the young,
compassionate with the aged,*

sympathetic with the striving,

and tolerant of the weak and the wrong.

*Sometime in your life, you will have been all of
these."*

· *George Washington Carver* ·

*"I do not ask the wounded person how he feels;
I, myself, become the wounded person."*

· *Walt Whitman* ·

There is a brilliant anecdote shared by Andrew J. Bracevich at the outset of his book, "Breach of Trust."[11] He describes the July 4 homecoming of Bridget Lydon, a young Boston area sailor, to Fenway Park. In what he deems a "theatrical production" put on by the Red Sox and the Pentagon, he describes a pregame spectacle of American flags, the U.S. Marine Corps choral ensemble, and a flyover by U.S. Air Force F-15C Eagles—the crowd roaring in approval. The Lydon family gathered around the pitcher's mound as a prerecorded message from

---

[11] Andrew J. Bracevich. *Breach of Trust: How Americans Failed Their Soldiers and Their Country* (Picador: 2013).

Bridget was aired on the Jumbotron, creating the appearance that she was still overseas. But, in a carefully staged twist, the young woman then appeared in person, a joyful reunion shared in and celebrated with the screams of the crowd in attendance.

It was not just an act of kindness for the sailor and her family, Bracevich points out; it was also a carefully staged PR event from which both the Red Sox organization and the Pentagon walked away looking triumphant.

The paradox of such a display, the author writes, is this: "In recent decades, an injunction to 'support the troops' has emerged as [a] central tenet. Since 9/11 this imperative has become, if anything, even more binding. Indeed, as citizens, Americans today acknowledge no higher obligation." All well and good, right? The problem, he underlines, is in the fulfillment of this obligation. While a noble few have chosen to do so concretely by enlisting in the armed forces or undertaking to directly serve the troops in some way, most Americans, he says, have "settled for symbolism," as the masses in general "resist any definition of civic duty that threatens to crimp lifestyles."

While WWII era America sought to do everything it could to support the war effort—average citizens sending their binoculars overseas for use by the Navy, mothers nationwide serving their babies rice cereal to conserve wheat for the troops—in contrast today, such brief and passive sympathetic displays as the July 4 Fenway Park spectacle seem, to most civilians, to be sufficient. "The message that citizens wish to convey to their soldiers is this," writes Bracevich: "although choosing not to be *with* you, we are still *for* you (so long as being for you entails nothing on our part). Cheering for the troops, in effect, provides a convenient mechanism for voiding obligation and perhaps easing guilty consciences."

This is not written to be an indictment of the well-meaning citizens who shared in the respectful and joyful display of patriotism that July 4 at Fenway Park, nor is it intended to undermine the good intentions of the millions of Americans who publicly voice their support of our military on a daily basis. What it is intended illustrate, rather, is the subtle but critical difference between sympathy and empathy.

Sympathy says to the troops and their families: "Thank you for your service and sacrifice." Empathy, however, says, "I see all that you are sacrificing to serve our country. I can only imagine what it feels like to be in your shoes. What can I do to help you?" For some empathetic Americans like Pat Tillman, who famously abandoned an NFL career to enlist and become an Army Ranger after 9/11, the answer is concrete action. For others, it is devoting time, efforts, funds, goods, and services to charitable organizations working to support the troops. Even conscientious efforts towards community improvement—in the spirit of enriching the country that our military seeks to defend—all of these things, born of empathy, matter.

It is relatively easy to sympathize, but empathy can at times be more difficult to muster. Sympathy requires no action, and little to no thought; it can be accomplished with the utterance of a few words. Empathy is more challenging; it requires us to think, and it puts us to work. For many of us who say things like, "I can't imagine what it is like to...," it is a struggle to empathize. Still, empathy need not elude us; it can be achieved by following a simple formula:

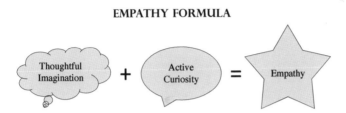

EMPATHY FORMULA

Thoughtful imagination is the ability to think realistically about a situation. Thoughtful imagination says: "I can imagine that it might be like this". However, that imagination must be checked by active curiosity. Active curiosity takes the above statement one step further and asks to those experiencing the situation: "Is that correct?", or "Did I get the right?" to confirm or deny the hypothesis. This simple formula allows us to put ourselves in another's shoes—and from there, we can begin developing real solutions.

The problem with sympathy is that it is passive—and if this book consciously holds one bias, it is a bias towards action. In the words of Nobel Laureate Jody Williams, "Tears without action are wasted sentiment." Sympathy is a first step, but it is empathy that ultimately makes the world a better place. It says, "I see your suffering and I feel and understand your pain," but then it asks: "What can I do to help?"

Showing sympathy makes others feel good;
Having empathy can make others better.

XV. ENERGY VS. EFFORT

"Don't get emotional in the ring. Stay cool; calm.
Use your mind like you're playing chess.
When you lose it, you're like Kamikaze.
You'll land one good shot, but get killed in order to
do it."

• *Carlos Vasquez* •

When it's fight night and Floyd Mayweather is taking to
the ring at the MGM Grand in his hometown of Las
Vegas, the mood is electric. By the time the sellout fight
begins, the arena will have met its maximum capacity of
over 17,000 people. Depending on who is fighting,
loyalties are often divided by international lines, and the
rivalry permeates the entire crowd. Spectators hype each
other up, draped in their countries' flags, drunk on Vegas
and high on the anticipation of combat. Flashing lights,
pounding music, bloody undercard fights, beautiful ring
girls, and celebrity spectators dripping in diamonds; the
adrenaline of the moment is palpable.

But then there is Floyd Mayweather, the man of the hour,
habitually and without exception cool as ice. "Oh, it's just
another day," he says of fight night; "I mean, it's work.
You know."[12] When he uttered these words, he was

---

[12] DIRECTV, "Exclusive Pre-Fight Interview: Mayweather,"
Filmed 4/2013. YouTube video, 3:00. Posted 4/2013.
https://www.bing.com/videos/search?q=exclusive+prefight+int

getting ready to defeat Robert Guerrero by unanimous decision, making him 44-0 as a professional boxer; he would retire from boxing four years later with a flawless professional record of 50-0 while leaving everyone around him wondering how he did it.

There is no more pure form competition than one-on-one human combat. All the hype in the world can't cover for you; when you're in the ring (or the cage), it's time to put up or shut up. One has to imagine that, no matter who you are—Floyd Mayweather or not—the closer you get to that 50-0, the more pressure is on your shoulders to win at all costs. Losing that 0 could cost you everything. And even under that pressure and on that stage, Mayweather has delivered again and again in a way that no other fighter in this era has managed to do.

If the formula to his success were easy to emulate, there would be other fighters out there boasting the same record—but there aren't. What we can recognize, from the field of Special Operations, is that Mayweather himself has cracked the same code that most Special Operators need to master, as well: the ability to differentiate between energy and effort.

Energy is the vibe in the MGM grand on fight night. It is the football team that bursts from the locker room in a cloud of smoke to cheering fans and pompoms. It is the celebratory dance; the smacks on the behind; the jumping on each other in the huddle.

---

erview+mayweather&view=detail&mid=03B21139B04287DB 44FD03B21139B04287DB44FD&FORM=VIRE.

It may be exhilarating for fans and athletes alike, but as far as securing the win goes? It establishes nothing.

In the world of Special Operations, where Operators must perform no-fail missions in life-or-death situations, it is understood what the fighter in the ring also knows: out of control emotions are a hindrance; not a help. Expending energy intentionally getting "hyped up"? It's all emotional—and emotions, for the most part, are not tactical. What Special Operators learn in these high-pressure tactical situations is that emotions will almost always distract from the task at hand.

Even still, many professional and amateur athletes believe that over-the-top displays of emotion show that they care about their sport, fans, and performance. What they fail to recognize is that true care is shown through action; not animation. Having an action plan, executing that plan, adapting as needed, and resetting to execute again—it doesn't sound sexy or exciting, but that is what care really looks like in practice. Watch the best in the world execute: they react to failure like they have seen it before and overcome it; they react to success like they have seen it before and will see it again.

Pressure to perform spikes the adrenaline response in human beings, whether in the boxing ring or on the battlefield. So does excitement. Wherever, whenever, and however this adrenaline response is initiated, we become more primal as a result. Our intellectual capacities and fine motor skills diminish as our gross motor skills take the forefront—not optimal in any combat scenario, whether in a ring at the MGM Grand, a battlefield in Afghanistan, or any other fight you can imagine.

In the world of Special Operations, it is widely understood that primal and tactical behavior are two very different things, and that they are in most ways diametrically opposed. As such, deliberate efforts are made in training to perform under self-induced stress. It is called "stress inoculation"—yes, like a vaccine. As Mayweather often says, fight night is like just another day at the office; Special Operators feel the same way. This attitude isn't cavalier; it's tactical. They all experience the same "butterflies" and "nerves" that anyone has before undertaking a fight, game, battle, or presentation. The difference in their case is that they focus that energy on the task at hand: not on hooting, hollering, and dancing, but on the effort that is required to reach the objective. Winning—whatever the contest.

And so, when Mayweather finally takes to the ring, walking out with his team to the music of his choice in a fanfare deliberately designed to maximize the energy of the crowd, his face will be calm and composed. His entire demeanor speaks to what he routinely professes: everything about this fight, even the walkout, is business as usual. Just another day at the office.

Among a team of Rangers on the helo headed out to a mission, you will find the same thing. Composure and focus. When success is achieved and an objective is seized, there is no chest bumping or slapping behinds. The focus remains on the effort. When Rangers take an objective, there is minimal celebration because all they've done, in their eyes, is their job. Winning was what they were supposed to do. They never considered any other outcome.

At the end of the day, no one is going to accuse Floyd Mayweather or a team of Rangers of lacking effort. What their efforts lack in dramatic flair, they make up for in calculating composure. His early rounds spent with restraint, slipping punches while stalking an opponent, measuring his jabs, and finding an opponent's weaknesses before picking him apart with surgical precision; Mayweather is often accused of being a "boring" fighter—his fights aren't exciting enough, critics say. They accuse him of going for the safe win instead of the knockout. But what Mayweather lacks in the dramatic flair of a knockout artist, he embodies as each of his fights becomes a masterclass in tactical performance under pressure. Military operations are rarely if ever executed with the dramatic flair of a Hollywood blockbuster, but what matters isn't that they're exciting; it's that objectives are achieved.

The lesson? Do not mistake energy for effort. Maximum effort need not be accompanied by great fanfare, and it can sometimes be less than exciting to observe as a spectator. Still, when you're the one who is pushing to prevail, it is critical to recognize that while energy looks thrilling, fun, and entertaining, it is actually effort—focused, composed, tactical effort—that is going to score you the win.

Do not mistake energy for effort.

Energy ⇒ diffuse
Effort ⇒ focused

XVI. RESPECT VS. CONSIDERATION

"In the midst of a culture that glorifies indulgent self-expression,
we may find that when we have the strength to engage in
considerate listening, we are in fact expressing ourselves at our best."
• P.M. Forni •

"A crucial measure of our success in life is the way
we treat one another
every day of our lives."
• P.M. Forni •

"We must be as courteous to a man as we are to a picture,
which we are willing to give the advantage of a good light."
• P.M. Forni •

Facebook. One of the greatest means of connecting human beings that the planet has ever seen and yet, it is often joked, we use it to look at cute videos of animals—and argue with one another.

It is a joke, but its meaning rings true. Perhaps we have always been this way, or perhaps social media has helped this trend along; whatever the case, we live in an environment which reinforces a negative communication landscape. Our habit has become to listen to argue, rather than listening to understand.

How often have we all done this? Think of a television news show, when a panel of "experts" with conflicting points of view are hosted for no real reason other than to argue. Do they ever sit and thoughtfully consider one another's opinions? Part with sincere expressions of newfound mutual respect?

Hardly; this isn't what excites the crowd and boosts ratings. These people are brought on TV to argue, and we buy into it. We hang on their every word as they listen to each other with the full intent of rebutting one another— often performing poorly on a rational level, spouting more emotionally-charged reactions than thoughtful responses.

Social media, where we communicate in small bursts that force us to keep our messages succinct, encourages us to do the same. Reacting to messages devoid of facial cues and vocal inflection, we infer meaning into what we read, and we may or not be right. Feelings get hurt, emotions run high, and real-world relationships often suffer real world damage over these petty cyber-battles. The other ill encouraged by social media is that it encourages a very self-focused form of expression. Instagram, Facebook, Snapchat, and Twitter posts are about us; they are one-sided and self-focused, encouraging us to concern ourselves with others only insofar as their impressions of us are concerned.

Living in this landscape where social media is a primary form of communication, the prospect for meaningful social interaction appears bleak at times. Our key, in making the best positive use of these tools while avoiding their pitfalls, is to focus on encouraging the values that social media discourages. To ask one another to worry less about sympathy ("Praying for [insert location of most recent mass shooting here]") and more about empathy (sending someone a private message or, better yet, giving them a call, and asking "How can I help?"). Less about identifying problems (becoming outraged at clickbait), and more about solving them (stop making the interesting important). To be less focused on sharing opinions (status update rants), and more interested in hearing them.

Most critically, in all of this chaos, we have lost our grip on one of the most distinctive characteristics of all civilized human interaction: consideration.

What ever happened to showing consideration for others? We often hang on the term "respect," instead. Perhaps most commonly heard is the term "disrespect," used especially as a verb. Feeling "disrespected" is the new righteous indignation. But when we say this is happening, is it really what we are feeling?

Respect is ritualistic. It is shown to offices, for example. Stand when the President of the United States enters the room; it doesn't matter who is President, nor is party or platform relevant. All stand. The same when the judge enters the courtroom: "All rise."

When an elderly person or a pregnant woman gets on a crowded subway and is not offered a seat, is this disrespect? Or is it a lack of consideration? And why does the distinction even matter?

Because, while respect is ritualistic and formulaic, consideration is action shown that considers another person's circumstances and feelings. It is considerate to think to oneself, "I have no problem standing; I am going to offer that elderly man / exhausted pregnant mom my seat, so that they can get off their feet." Consideration is not a reflection of obligation; it is the product of empathy. It is doing something not because you have to, but because you want to—out of consideration for another human being's feelings.

If we are not first empathetic, we cannot be considerate. If I don't pause to ask myself what my former college roommate might be feeling when she posts a political rant on her Facebook page, I will not respond with a compassionate, thoughtful, well-reasoned message that cuts to the heart of the matter. Is Facebook even the appropriate place to have such an important discussion? Perhaps an actual phone call or—better yet, a coffee date—would be in order. Consideration may ask, "What is this person going through that caused her to fly off the handle like that? Maybe, instead of engaging in a political battle, I should reach out privately and see what is going on in her life. Maybe she has other needs that are not being met." At its very best, consideration is looking for those needs and then trying to meet them.

Consideration may not always need to be so deeply involved of a process, though. It can also be just choosing to acknowledge that another person's feelings matter. A hot button topic of late has been the gender pronoun, as more and more people are choosing to request that others acknowledge them with their pronoun of choice. Feeling that their own rights or beliefs are infringed upon by this simple request, there are people who stalwartly refuse to do so. "If you are born a he, I'm calling you he," is their mindset. Fair and—this may sound controversial—not disrespectful to choose not to employ someone else's preferred gender pronoun.

HOWEVER.

It is a deeply inconsiderate action. By choosing not to use someone's preferred gender pronoun, what you are saying to them is, "Your feelings don't matter to me." It is a harsh statement to say to any other human being, especially when it costs you nothing (but perhaps your pride) to use their pronoun of choice. What are we really doing when we are being willfully inconsiderate? There is hardly a better definition of passive aggression. Knowing what would be the considerate thing to do, and choosing not to do it even when it costs us nothing, is quite literally weaponizing our capacity to be inconsiderate in order to indirectly harm someone else. It is a cowardly, hurtful, and unnecessarily divisive thing to do.

Still, there are elements of society which would have us feel justified in behaving this way. We live an age of the "f*** your feelings" movement. In fact, there is a somewhat popular book by that very title. Indeed, for many of us who have worked in professions or gone after athletic pursuits that require a high level of mental toughness, we have invested a great deal of effort into learning to strategically suppress our own emotions in order to complete tasks that do not come intuitively to us. Jumping out of perfectly good airplanes. Locking ourselves into octagonal cages to consensually fight someone who wants to knock us out. Running ultramarathons. There is even a great deal of mental toughness involved in getting back to the gym for the first time after a long hiatus. It is never easy. We have to override and suppress or redirect our emotions in order to reach our goals.

Having or developing the capacity to strategically tell ourselves to "f*** our feelings," however, does not make the wholesale dismissal of other people's feelings justifiable. When we charge through life in that mindset, it truly is like being the proverbial bull in a china shop: destructive to everyone around us. What good does it do anyone or anything? And what skin is it off our backs to simply use someone's preferred gender pronoun and move on? To show consideration for a complete stranger's feelings before insulting them on Twitter? Why is this even an issue?

Many people are fond of saying that "Respect isn't given; it's earned." Whether or not this is true for each of us is the choice of the individual, though there are going to be consequences for those of us who choose not to rise when the judge walks into the metaphorical courtroom. The Private who chooses *not* to drop and give his Drill Sergeant 20 is going to have to answer for that decision.

But try substituting the word "consideration" into that same framework. Imagine actually saying, "Consideration isn't given; it's earned." Imagine charging through life with the general rule of thumb that it is 100% acceptable to be inconsiderate to anyone and everyone until they give us good reason to think of their feelings before we act.

Absurd, right?

Just as importantly, we must pause before we allow ourselves to ever feel "disrespected." At the end of the day, what we are more likely feeling is that we wish someone else had been more considerate towards us. If that is the case, how can we ask for this? In many instances, the best way of asking for consideration is by *showing* it for others. By these means, we can reset our collective social and moral climate to recognize that sometimes, it is worth doing the right thing—simply because it is the right thing to do. Showing consideration for others is one of those things.

Consideration is the antidote to disrespect.

HABERE
ET
ESSE

(To Have and To Be)

XVII. TRUST

"The best way to find out if you can trust somebody
is to trust them."
∙ *Ernest Hemingway* ∙

Trust: is it earned or given?

Think about it in your own life. What is your knee-jerk
reaction?

For the majority of people, the response is invariably the
same: "Trust must be earned before it can be given!" It
seems rational to hold this belief. Wouldn't it make sense
to measure and assess an individual's trustworthiness
before placing our fate, or the fate of our business, in their
hands?

The problem is, though, that this is not how we actually
live our lives.

Have you ever flown in an airplane? Driven a car?
Received emergency medical treatment?

Consider each case individually. When you fly, do you
know your pilot's name? Marital status? Do you know

where he was trained to fly? Do you know if he's ever had a chemical dependency problem? If that feels like a stretch, think about your last visit to the ER. Before allowing her to render aid, did you stop your physician to ask where she went to medical school? Did you ask her what rank she finished in her class? How long she has interned or been a resident? How much do you really know in either case about these complete strangers who hold your life in their hands?

Maybe neither of these examples resonate. In that case, think about the last time you drove in your car. How far did you drive, and how long were you in the car? How many other people do you think came within your close proximity while you were on the road? After all, a car in motion can kill you at speeds as low as 15 mph. Did you know any of those people driving around you?

How much time, if any, did it take them to earn your trust?

Implicit trust

The truth of the matter is that it took them no time at all, because you trusted them implicitly. You had to; otherwise, you never would've set foot on the plane, allowed the doctor to make critical decisions on your behalf, or even taken a short drive around the corner this morning. Trust is implicit in many of our relationships with complete strangers every day; we just don't realize it. And if this is the case, we must ask ourselves: why should our working relationships be any different?

A good litmus test for the presence of implicit trust is to consider how you would feel if someone else did *not* perform the role that you expected of them. How would you feel if your pilot or physician showed up to work intoxicated? How do you feel when another driver erratically cuts you off and causes you to swerve into another lane?

It's infuriating. You feel wronged. And why? Because you TRUSTED them. You trusted those people to do the right thing. Through this optic, consider all of the other people you implicitly trust every day. The teacher who takes your child to the bathroom. The restaurant employees who prepare your food. The cashier who hands you your change (do you really count it every time?). The sky truly is the limit, to such an extent that it's possible to identify ways we implicitly trust almost everyone around us on a daily basis. Implicit trust informs a social contract of civility that forms the very foundation of most human societies around the world.

And yet, when we find ourselves in leadership roles, how quick we are to set the bar high for others to earn our trust—setting it highest for the people closest to us. Ernest Hemingway is reported to have once said that the best way to find out if you can trust somebody is to trust them. Indeed, as leaders, it is our responsibility to give trust. We must start by giving trust.

The pitfall? Human nature being what it is, every leader will inevitably get burned sometimes. Not everyone in whom you place your trust will turn out to have been worthy of it. What happens when trust is violated? A poor leader will do nothing. A good leader will emplace regulations to prevent the same offense from recurring. The great leader, however, will understand the unique nature of the offense. The great leader will recognize that the offender is a solitary individual, and take action steps to ensure that the same offense does not recur. What the great leader does not do is punish the whole group or revoke trust from everyone due just to the offense of one. That's kindergarten discipline: if Jimmy and Susie can't play nicely with the crayons, then *nobody* gets to use the crayons today. There's no place for that in a high-performance working environment.

Surely, however, some individuals must be innately more trustworthy than others. True?

Consider this story. There's a ladder in front of you, and you are tasked with climbing it. To your left is your best friend in the world; on your right, a complete stranger. You need someone to take your phone, money, wallet, and keys and hold them while you climb the ladder. Who do you hand them to?

Whatever your initial choice, consider this possibility. What if you hand them to whoever reaches out their hand first? It is a simple action, but it shows you the person who is sincerely trying to help. Anyone with combat experience can vouch for this: in combat, where both the best and worst that humanity can offer are at play, it quickly becomes evident that when someone is trying to help, they are probably a good person. A trustworthy person. Your knowledge of a person has no bearing upon

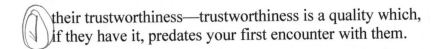their trustworthiness—trustworthiness is a quality which, if they have it, predates your first encounter with them.

What if the person with the outstretched hand decides to run off and abscond with your possessions? You must also trust that the other person will chase them down and bring them back. Even when one person turns out to not have been worthy of your trust, trust that others will still be good. You will usually be right.

There is no value in being jaded. When you assume all people are bad, you hold contempt for them. And when you hold someone in contempt, you cannot lead them. Why? Because you can only lead what you love. The highest form of love is acceptance, and it can be shown to anyone.

Remember this: managers manage things like resources, time, and commodities. Leaders don't manage; they love people and inspire them. Leaders give people hope and purpose, and none of these things are possible without first being preceded by trust.

Giving trust is no easy task, and can set you up for pain, but when we do it, our people are better, our organizations are better, and we are better.

When I was young, I thought that all men were good.

When I went to war, I thought that all men were evil.

Now, I realize that all men are just men.

XVIII. RESILIENCE

"You have power over your mind—not outside events.

Realize this, and you will find strength."

· *Marcus Aurelius* ·

"You see a lot of guys give up mentally,
and that's why they get knocked out or submitted.
They give up mentally before they lose."

· *Georges St. Pierre* ·

"The good Lord gave you a body that can stand most anything.

It's your mind you have to convince."

· *Vince Lombardi* ·

It's a football game: a big game, clutch time. Pressure and stakes are high. Teams face off on the defense's 15-yard line. The crowd yells at fever pitch, and the arena quivers with adrenaline and intensity. The ball is snapped, and bodies start to collide with both violence and strange beauty. The quarterback drops back, scanning for an open receiver. He sees his target...it looks perfect...a receiver wide open...in the endzone! He brings his arm back and attempts to pass for the touchdown his team desperately needs...and he fails, missing his mark by a long shot. Incomplete pass.

The QB smacks his helmet in frustration, rips open his chinstrap, and yells at the receiver. Overtaken with emotion, he loses his cool—and then his focus. Instead of taking the field goal, he tries another passing play, but throws the ball away again: his emotions drive him to play harder when he should be playing smarter.

Now, imagine a different scenario. Consider a small Special Operations Unit overseas, operating in a hostile environment. They move with stealth to their target, having already walked miles from the helicopter landing zone. Setting on the door with a confident knowledge that the target is just inside, they silently and carefully place a breaching charge to gain access to their building, where they will either kill or capture their desired target. In a flash of violence and perceived chaos, they breach the door and enter swiftly into the room, moving in unison to support each other as they survey their surroundings through green night vision for hidden enemies. As they clear the first room and move down a dark hallway, an armed combatant emerges from an open door, raising his rifle to shoot. The operator, as he's trained thousands of times to do, spots this target, takes the shot...and misses.

Does he unsling his weapon? Throw it down on the ground? Take off his helmet, storm out the door, and call it a day? Does he yell at anyone? Does he just stop what he is doing and react to the miss?

These questions don't even merit a response. Of *course* he doesn't. Like the quarterback discussed earlier, he practices regularly and is extremely good at what he does; he doesn't miss often. So, what does he do after his first miss? He takes the shot again. Missing once is an anomaly; the second shot should do it. But if he misses again?

Missing twice means that something is wrong – either with him, his equipment, or his environment. What has previously worked a thousand times now isn't working for some reason. Trying harder by taking the same shot again is not going to do the job. Knowing this, he immediately adjusts and adapts. Maybe he changes his sight picture, or perhaps he adjusts his angle, but he doesn't just stand there thinking about it. He doesn't react to anything. He acts to adapt the action to reach his desired outcome and to ensure his round reaches the target. There's no time for anything else when lives are hanging in the balance. The adjustments and the decisions must be made in a split second. And the ability to make those adjustments on the spot, immediately in the face of failure or malfunction, is the very picture of resilience.

What is the difference between this quarterback and the special operator? These are both highly trained professionals who have invested thousands of hours of training time into developing the capacity to perform their jobs under crushing levels of pressure. Why does one stagger where the other can continue to perform?

The only thing distinguishing each of these high performers from the other in these examples is their mental preparation. Overcome with emotion and reacting to his initial incomplete pass, the quarterback loses his focus and allows one mistake to snowball into other failed plays. The operator, on the other hand, remains controlled. First shot missed the mark? That's odd; I don't miss. Let's try this again. Second shot misses? Ok, something is off. Tweak something, readjust, and boom. Eliminate the threat and move on to the next room.

The critical mistake made by the quarterback is that he allows self-doubt to creep in. We all know what self-doubt is; it's a small, subtle voice that tells us when to quit. It could be a message from our body's screaming muscles ("I can't do any more burpees!"), or it could come from inside our mind before we even begin ("There's no way I could ever run a marathon!"). It also says, "You aren't good enough," or "You aren't trying hard enough." We all have this voice – this nagging, doubting voice. Whoever you are, and wherever it comes from, it is not the voice that matters; it is one's reaction to this voice that differentiates performance, and in some cases separates a quitter from someone who presses on.

Those who press on do so knowing that the voice is a liar.

Where does this voice of doubt come from? It's simply the fear of the unknown. Ask a group of athletes to do push-ups until you say they're done, and they'll start to act exhausted after the first ten or twenty. Tell them you need them to knock out fifty push-ups, and they'll come up with ways to crush them. The fear of the unknown is what tricks people into believing that they're not up for the task. The unknown lets the voice create false stories that influence our actions, or our inaction.

The other mistake made by the quarterback is that, in response to becoming emotional, he opts to try harder. It is true that in pursuits of sheer brute force, trying harder may indeed be effective. But more often than not, smart adaptations will gain you more ground. Much of life is like a game of chess—strategic and thoughtful. When you're a few moves away from being put in check mate, are you going to play chess harder? What would that even look like? Your only effective choice is to control your emotional reaction to stress, adapt, and play smarter.

Much of special operations training is successful because it forces individuals to see that this voice of self-doubt inside of them is an illusion. When you've time and time again pushed beyond what you thought was your breaking point, you start to learn that your body will do whatever you want it to. Your point of actual physical failure lies way outside the boundary of what that little voice will try to have you believe. Once you recognize this, you will come to understand your true capacity to complete any given task one way or the other. It might not be pretty and it might not break any records, but you WILL get the job done. And only those who have come to this understanding can shut down the voice for good.

What happens when the voice goes away? You are able to see individual failures as anomalies rather than indicators of personal limitations. It's a common fallacy to which we all fall victim in diverse parts of our lives: we make one mistake, even a mistake that's not really catastrophic, and we say to ourselves, "I'll never try *that* again." But why? If something worked 99% of the time before the one time it finally failed, that's not enough empirical evidence to tell you that it definitively doesn't work. Yet we live our lives this way all the time, quitting after a single failure.

We get one rejection letter and assume we were never cut out for that dream job—when it might just be that we were not cut out for that particular company. If we believe the voice of doubt, and jump to the conclusion that we were never cut out for the job, we may miss the simple adaptation that maybe the resume just needed a few tweaks.

And it is in this key moment, where we choose to adapt instead of quit, that resilience is born.

Adaptability and resilience are primal human concepts. The innovations that have allowed humanity to persist and thrive in some of the most remote corners of the globe are nothing more than the result of adaptability. This wooden spear isn't strong enough to pierce a bison's hide—let's try a stone arrowhead. Still not enough? We can get on horseback and chase the herd of bison off a cliff. There are ancient Native American artifacts depicting this very hunting practice, which allowed for the harvesting of the massive beasts whose bodies yielded critical food and supplies for tools, clothing, medicine, and shelter. It was a critical adaptation that enabled the survival of countless human beings.

Here is one thing to remember: while the tendency to adapt and be resilient is an innate human behavior, the inner voice of doubt is not. Consider the process of learning to walk: there is no documented case in history of a human child, physically capable of walking, who gave up on trying and never learned. Humans are not born like horses, walking shortly after birth, or even puppies, who can at least creep over to their mother's teat; we are born entirely helpless. Yet we all crawl, and we all eventually walk. Watch a baby learn to do these things, and see the determination, desire, and focus. Watch the child fall, take hard bumps, and get right back up again. No child has to be taught to do this.

As human beings, the ability to face challenges and learn through adaptation comes naturally to us. It's only as adults that we sometimes seem to forget this. Doubt creeps in, and it whispers to us that we can't. Silence the doubt, throttle emotion, and adapt with composure—this is mature resiliency. Remember always that the little voice of doubt is a liar. When we do this, our resiliency—and capacity for greatness—expands exponentially.

Embracing the suck is about loving your fate: accepting where you are, and having a plan to move forward.

XIX. INITIATIVE

"Beaten paths are for beaten men."

• Eric Johnston •

"Seize the initiative in whatever you undertake.
Consider fully, act decisively.
Know when to stop."
• Jigoro Kano •

"Think outside the box."

It's a business world catchphrase that's become so ubiquitous that it wavers on the edge of cliché. What are we really asking people for when we use it?

Yes, we want innovation. We are seeking ideas that are not so obvious to have occurred to us already. And, of course, we want creativity.

But, like inspiration and so many other most prized human capabilities, creativity and innovation cannot be forced. No one can be made to take initiative, because initiative, by definition, implies self-starting. Initiative has to arise organically, and in order for it to arise, only one primary thing is necessary: freedom.

Now, two suggestions. Think of which statement from a team leader would inspire a greater sense of freedom: "Think outside the box." Or, "I'm going to give you four parameters. Within these four parameters, literally anything else goes. I'm curious to see what you come up with."

horizon *Frontiers* *destination*

What those of the "think outside the box" mentality get wrong is that high performers don't need to be pushed outside of the box. Outside of the box is where they already live. To them, the world is a great frontier of possibility—and if you are leading a high performing team, all your people actually need are parameters: simple, clear guidelines of how they know it is time to pull back.

Still, this idea isn't just for high performing teams; it also helps those not predisposed to innovation by providing a path, direction, and azimuth. It helps give a map to those who don't really know where to start. People who have been instructed to generally just "think outside the box" can become paralyzed by the countless options they find themselves confronting. It is Hick's Law in a nutshell—as the number of choices is increased, human decision-making time also increases logarithmically. People don't always need to be told what to do or how to do it, but providing them with at least some direction is always important. As one military leader succinctly puts it, "I don't tell my people to think outside the box; I tell them to think *inside* the box. There are only four boundaries they can't cross: the legal, safe, ethical, and moral. As long as their idea falls within those four categories, I welcome it."

Human history is rife with examples of parameters as guides for behavior. Ancient masters of martial arts understood this especially well, and that is why so many martial arts disciplines include succinct, simple, and memorable guidelines. Consider the ancient Tanseki School of Swordsmanship, governed by three prohibitions only: to give up, to misbehave, or to be clumsy.[13] Three precepts, but just enough to insulate a warrior from disaster while allowing him the necessary agility to remain adaptable in battle. The guiding principle is to provide direction, but never be too prescriptive. Giving too much direction stifles innovation, and can stop people before they start. In cases where the direction is overbearing, most solutions will be limited by whoever is providing the guidance.

Another illustration, perhaps more intuitive, comes from the common experience of parenting. Think of every rule that you have for your children, or every rule under which you operated as a child. Now, imagine three parameters: dangerous, disrespectful to others, and disrespectful to property. Nearly everything we ask our children not to do falls inside the boundaries of these three parameters. So, what if children are encouraged to ask themselves— before acting— "Is what I am about to do safe? Is it disrespectful to others? Am I going to break or destroy something?" Implementing them is an effective parenting

---

[13] John Stevens, *Budo Secrets: Teachings of the Martial Arts Masters* (Boston: Shambhala, 2002).

tool, and a way to teach children accountability, as they learn to ask themselves if their actions fall within these guidelines. When a child makes a misstep, a parent can ask them, "What went wrong here?" and they can analyze for themselves where they should've better thought things through. The most beautiful part about it is that within these parameters, children's creativity is free to blossom unstifled as far as their imaginations can carry them.

This is because parameters do not fence us in; rather, they allow absolute freedom as we safely exist within their bounds, and it is the creativity and innovation born of freedom that we are really seeking when we ask people to "think outside the box." The truth is that it is actually thinking *inside* the box—the parameters of the absolutely unacceptable—that will enable our team's creativity by maximizing their freedom. The parameters should not be seen as absolute boundaries, but as merely guideposts that help achieve something yet unimagined.

When trying to build initiative, guidance should be a 'how to'—not a 'what to.'

XX. COURAGE

"Courage is resistance to fear, mastery of fear, not absence of fear."

• *Mark Twain* •

"F*** fear."

• *Tony Blauer* •

Fixed versus growth mindset: the principles by which we choose to define much of how we see ourselves. Fixed mindset, psychologists tell us, can be dangerous because it stunts our personal growth. If we see our qualities as fixed, we fail to recognize the power that we have to change them. Notwithstanding, we characterize ourselves and one another in such absolute terms as "I'm not good with numbers," or "I'm no athlete," without realizing that none of these subjective classifications are outside our control in the way that actual innate characteristics— being 5'10", having blue eyes—truly are.

When it comes to courage, this is where we often find ourselves. We think of the quality of being courageous as if it were fixed at the time of our birth. As such, we tend to reserve it for someone other than ourselves, and we don't tend to think of courage as a developable characteristic. We honor the courage of our troops overseas, imagining that they possess some innate difference of character that we lack.

Growth mindset is something different. When we are
operating within this paradigm, we understand that what
we are not now, we may still one day become. As such,
our absolutist statements of self-doubt can evolve into
something more akin to: "I am not currently adept at X,
but with time and practice, I can be." This is the formula
for growth mindset, and it is applicable to almost
everything. Students who can adopt this way of thinking
are proven to be more persistent; children who are raised
to think in these terms show more positive psychological
outcomes. And, when it comes to courage, it is essential
that we learn to think in this way.

The connection is not coincidental. Our children, like our
teams and our people, come to believe that they are who
we tell them they are. If their accomplishments are met
with absolute statements like, "How brave you are!" they
begin to relate their successes to their sense of their own
innate intelligence. This takes a damaging turn when they
fail, because when successes are attributed to innate
qualities, they attribute their own failures to lacking the
same. "How brave I am" quickly devolves into "No
matter how hard I try, I will never be brave enough."
However, when we praise effort, we are praising an aspect
that they can control. In doing so, we change a fixed
mindset to a growth mindset. In the face of failure, "I will
never be brave enough" becomes "I can be brave if I try
hard enough." We can create courage in our children—or
our teams—simply by changing the focus of their success.

There is a second key element to creating courage in
others: by giving them a sense of hope and trust. To do so,

we must instill in them the hope that what they are doing is both good and worthwhile; hope that they have it in them to succeed. We must give them reason to trust that we will be there to resource them, support them, and catch them if they falter. When we provide hope and trust, it can give anyone the courage to accomplish any task.

Hope and trust. To some, they may seem like weak words. Not what one might expect to hear from an Army Ranger; not what Hollywood and popular media would have us believe of our nation's warriors. But believe this: there are few things that every person needs in this life, and hope and trust are two of the most essential. The toughest, roughest, most grizzled person you know; they, too, require hope and want trust. We all do—it is a natural part of the human condition. Any time we think of the future, and anticipate another day, we are hoping. And any time we are acting on faith in another human being—giving them our confidence, or earning theirs—we are trusting. When hope and trust die, all that is human in us cannot survive.

Regardless of whether or not you believe yourself to be courageous, courage is your responsibility, and it is a capacity that you have. How is this even possible? Because courage is not the absence of fear. It is acting in the face of fear. Acting in *spite* of fear. The real "superpower" of the Special Operations door kicker overseas is not that he is fearless; it is that he sees the door, feels the fear of what may be awaiting him on the other side, and moves forward anyway. Fear be damned.

Coach Tony Blauer understands this, as he's coached everyone from tier one military personnel to concerned civilian citizens on the psychology of fear for decades. Thousands of hours of research and real-world experience consistently pointed him to the same conclusion when he developed his "cycle of fear": fear is a liar. It is—to employ Blauer's acronym—nothing more than False Evidence Appearing Real, or False Expectations Appearing Real. Fear tells us that something cannot be done, and when most of us hear the voice of fear inside, our mistake is that we believe it. We fail to realize that those people we see as superheroes—the ones who seem to have no fear, and all the courage in the world—are human beings who feel the same fears that we do. They have just learned to ignore it. And that's actually all it takes to have courage.

As leaders, we have the responsibility to build courage in our people. We must assist them in adopting the growth mindset which says "I can be courageous by choosing to act in spite of fear." Courage is not an absolute trait with which we are born; it is 100% developable, and it can be achieved in an instant when we learn to dismantle and disregard the fears that are holding us back.

Where there is no courage
There is no hope
There is no trust
Where there is no hope
Where there is no trust
There is only
Death

DUCATUS

(Leadership)

XXI. WHAT ARE YOU LEADING FOR?

"What is necessary to change a person is to change his awareness of himself."

· *Abraham Maslow* ·

What is a good leader? The question is almost unanswerable. It is easiest to just acquiesce and say that it is situationally dependent. "The right person, the right environment, and the right situation," many conclude. Still, this is hardly a roadmap for success; it is more a simple characterization of the perfect storm of circumstances that may help to enable effective leadership—little more.

According to the previous, common definition, good leadership is circumstantial. But what happens when it is viewed along the lines of a progression, akin to that of Maslow's hierarchy of needs? In Maslow's model, human fulfillment is achieved progressively: first when basic, concrete needs are met (food, water, etc.), but ultimately culminating when the abstract needs of self-actualization are met.

Leadership, according to the Prodromos Evolution of Leadership model, follows a similar progression, each facet building upon the previous one until the highest level is reached. Still, while Maslow's hierarchy becomes increasingly self-focused as one moves up the pyramid, the Prodromos model asks the leader to look outside him or herself to reach the highest levels of achievement.

THE PRODROMOS EVOLUTION OF LEADERSHIP©2016[14]

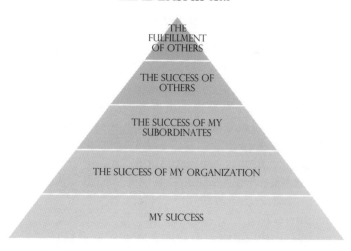

The model looks like this. In its most lowly form, leadership is entirely self-focused; the leader is only worried about her own well-being and success. On level two, the leader is now focused on organizational success, even at the possible immediate expense of the employees or others associated with the organization. Level three sees the leader become concerned with the success of his subordinates, making sure that they are advancing and doing well in the organization. Most people stop at this level.

---

[14] JC Glick and Sarah Ngu, *A Light in the Darkness: Leadership Development for the Unknown* (Lightning Press: 2017).

Still, there are two more levels to go. At level four, the leader reaches a more enlightened perspective when it comes to her subordinates, because she is now focused on their success—even if it comes before her own. It is an incredibly selfless and true form of leadership, but it still ultimately prioritizes the well-being of the organization, leader, and others.

Level five of the Prodoromos model is the highest form of leadership because it is entirely focused on the fulfillment and wellbeing of others. At this level, the leader considers the needs of each individual on his team over the needs of anything else—including the organization of which they are a part. Such a leader may even encourage a standout employee to venture out of the organization to seek a better position for himself, even though it may hurt the organization. As opposed to self-interest, this highest form of leadership is entirely focused on "other-interest."

With the Prodromos Evolution of Leadership model in hand, any leader should be able to define where they are in the progression, allowing them to self-assess and devise their own plan to move higher. Even so, while the model is hierarchical, it allows for the situational and environmental aspects of leadership, and not every level need necessarily be reached sequentially. For example, there may be times that a leader needs to be solely concerned with the organization's survival in order to ensure work for others in the future. The task may be organizationally focused at times, but under ideal circumstances, the target outcome is always other-focused.

Some will read this and ask why a leadership model would prioritize people over organizations. But, as our chapters on loyalty and empathy will have one recall, as leaders, we must always remember that our people come first. At the end of the day, though not every organization is about people, people are the sole purpose of leadership. Whether an athletic team, a military unit, a family, a small startup or a Fortune 500 company—organizations are not always made for and by people, but people are the only reason for leadership. For this reason—which should become clear throughout the course of this book—leadership must always remain people-focused in order to be effective.

Effective leadership puts people first.

XXII. CHARACTERISTICS OF A LEADER

"Be gentle and you can be bold;
be frugal and you can be liberal;
avoid putting yourself before others
and you can become a leader among men."

⋅ *Lao Tzu* ⋅

What are the characteristics of a "leader"? It depends upon how you define the word. Even a violent dictator can control, but obedience by compulsory force is not the same thing as the special breed of willful, inspired commitment that a true leader evokes.

For hundreds and even thousands of years, the prevailing view of leadership has been that its definitive qualities should be dominance and strength. As one scholar said of the theories of leadership put forth in Plato's Republic, "Plato thinks that there are naturally lion-like men who should by rights rule. He also disturbingly sees democracy as a hindrance to these lion-like men taking their rightful position in the world...and his ideal of the strong resourceful ruthless man of affairs was very admired in Plato's day."[15] To attempt to dismantle that Platonic view

---

[15] Angela Hobbs. "Honor, Courage, Thumos, and Plato's Idea of Greek Manliness." *The Art of Manliness.* Podcast audio, 12/5/16.

on leadership would be a book—volumes, really—in and of itself. What this example better serves to illustrate is that there has always been a perception of leadership as being an expression of dominance. Still, through experience—and the experience of some notable others—this one-dimensional perception need not endure. In fact, the type of leadership which solicits willful engagement from those who are led requires far softer and more "humanistic" attributes.

Just about 500 years after Plato died, Marcus Aurelius was born. Aurelius was raised by an adoptive father—emperor Antoninus Pius—and at the outset of the Meditations, he describes his adoptive father's skillful qualities as a leader. Among the attributes that Aurelius observes: Antoninus Pius bore a "complete indifference to meretricious honours;" he had "willingness to listen to any project for the common good." He dismissed no question on "cursory first impression," but rather "painstakingly and patiently examined" them all. His friendships were "enduring;" neither "capricious" nor "extravagant," and "his friends were under no obligation to join him at his table…when they were detained by other engagements, it made no difference to him." He was "impervious to flattery," and with regard to others, "no hint of jealousy showed in his prompt recognition of outstanding abilities." Habitually, he would "weigh every incident, taking his time about it, calmly, methodically, decisively, and consistently."[16]

---

[16] Marcus Aurelius, *Meditations*, Transl. Maxwell Staniforth (Penguin: 2005).

From his son's assessment, Antoninus Pius' strengths as a leader emerge to fall under four major headings—none of which are a customary expression of dominance, but rather of connection. The strengths which his famed son chose to immortalize in the Meditations center around four key areas: empathy, loyalty, humility, and curiosity. In his friendships, Pius was loyal and empathetic. In processing information and making decisions, he was humble and curious. In private choices, he was humble; publicly, he also had the humility and curiosity to learn from others and take their guidance.

Of all the characteristics that his son—a very powerful man in his own right—could have chosen to emphasize, the virtues of empathy, loyalty, humility, and curiosity permeate a nuanced portrait of Pius' leadership style that extends far beyond a statement of his grandeur and well-suitedness to rule. Instead, it speaks to an understanding that the best kind of leadership is far more complex than mere dominance, and it is deeply rooted in personal virtues. A closer look at each of them:

LOYALTY

Our military often talks about loyalty to laws, ideals, organizations, and country. These are all positives, but this misses a critical factor: without loyalty to people, all of these things fall by the wayside. Consider them one by one. When laws are created, they must be loyal to the people they serve, or they will create more misery than order. While laws might be stable, ideals can shift and morph over time; loyalty to an ideal can be dangerous, as an ideal can take on a life of its own and lead people astray. Loyalty to an organization isn't productive; organizations are mindless entities that can't give loyalty back. As for loyalty to country, it only takes a moment to look at what a country really is and realize that we are not so much loyal to a piece of ground as we are to the people who occupy it. This is the very source of conflict in parts of the world where artificial post-war boundaries have been drawn: these lines in the sand do nothing to divide unified groups of people who remain loyal to one another despite what geographical space they occupy.

When we, as leaders, are first loyal to our people, we will start to ask ourselves the right questions. How are we taking care of, looking out for, and prioritizing them? Our job is to develop them, make them better, and underwrite their mistakes. In "A Light in the Darkness,"[17] the point is made that our people's mistakes should not just be accepted; they should be celebrated, because they are indicators that our people are learning and trying to innovate. It is all a matter of perspective, and the right things come into focus when we remain people-centered in our loyalty.

What does it look like when leaders are not loyal to their people? The first thing that flies out the window is loyalty to the leader. Loyalty—or lack thereof—is reciprocal. When a leader is disloyal, people will be loyal to no one but themselves. But if you take care of your people like you mean it, reciprocal loyalty is the dividend. Case in point: the Ranger Regiment makes a point of taking care of their people on a level rarely seen in most organizations. A Ranger's child gets sick during the night, and the Ranger

---

[17] JC Glick and Sarah Ngu, *A Light in the Darkness: Leadership Development for the Unknown* (Lightning Press: 2017).

doc will have her pre-triaged and met in the ER. A Ranger loses an ID card on Saturday, and someone will come in to make a new card over the weekend to ensure no disruption when that Ranger reports to work on Monday. This type of unrelenting loyalty pays off: when you are good to people and you take care of them, there is nothing that they will not do for you and your organization. As they and their families are taken care of, they will show equal consideration to you and your organization.

This is critical, because it is key to remember: the leader's job is not the final action or the outcome of the organization's purpose. The leader's job is to take care of the *people* who are responsible to ensure the outcome of the organization. Understanding this principle can keep any leader oriented in the right direction.

HUMILITY

How many times have we all heard the phrase, "honored and humbled"? The pairing is so ubiquitous that we tend to think along these lines: that to be humble is to avoid being prideful or boastful in the face of greatness. But humility in leadership is something more, and it is perhaps less glamorous. It is to willingly take a backseat to others' ideas; to say, "It doesn't have to be done my way." Humility in leadership is the open-mindedness to recognize that the leader in charge may have the last say, but it is also her duty to make sure that other voices are heard. Recall Marcus Aurelius' praise of his father Pius: that he was "willing to listen to any project for the common good."

An organization which is exclusively directed by its leader will only ever be as good as one individual – that leader directing it. The leader serves as the stopping point for what that organization can achieve. By the same token, an organization which hears all voices and considers input regardless of the source opens itself to innovation and growth that expands far beyond the reaches of a single human mind.

Humble leaders remember that they are not the best; they are the best available. There is always someone better out there—and they could be hiding in one's own organization. If one is not harnessing and leveraging every resource of their organization in every way possible, how are they a good leader? It is key for every leader to remember that their people are the most important resource that they have. Again, as Aurelius spoke of Pius: "No hint of jealousy showed in his prompt recognition of outstanding abilities, whether in public speaking, law, ethics, or any other department, and he took pains to give each man the chance of earning a reputation in his own field." This is humility.

CURIOSITY

Leaders tend to fall out of touch with their own organizations for two reasons. Some, lacking all humility, think that they already have all the answers. Others, afraid of looking like they don't know the answers already, never ask the right questions. Either way, the endgame is the same: leaders lose track, and they can't right the ship. The best leaders, however, are unabashedly curious. They ask questions: not because they feel like they should, but because they truly want to hear the answers. When something goes wrong, a good leader is genuinely curious about what went wrong, not "who did the wrong thing", but truly what led to the failure.

There is also the matter of "yes men." Many people try to read into their leader's questions, parrot what they think their leader wants to hear. The only way to avoid this is to ask questions in an authentic way, in order to get authentic answers. People need to know that this is what you want and need from them, and your authenticity gives them permission to be authentic with you in return.

EMPATHY

Having empathy means having an active understanding of your people. It is putting yourself in their shoes, and being able to understand how your own decisions will affect them. An empathetic leader can understand and temper their people's workload and the task organization, but only after they have sat down and really thought about what their people are going through, and what the task will really be like for them. Empathy also means that the leader hears their people's feedback, and actively tries to understand why they feel the way that they do about the tasks they are being asked to complete.

There is a popular saying in military circles: "embrace the suck." This is a good thing to do—when you're the one experiencing the suck! When your team is suffering through it, though, your job has nothing to do with embracing the suck. You are instead called upon to understand the suck to which they have been subjected, and this is not always an easy task. Understanding what it is like to be a woman going through Ranger school, for example, may be a stretch for many males. Empathy means putting yourself in their shoes, understanding *their* suck, and making decisions with this knowledge under your belt.

Leaders who fail to empathize stand an enormous risk of abusing their people, in turn losing their faith and trust. When people feel unheard, they don't feel understood—and how can a leader give people hope when the leader doesn't even understand who his people are? As importantly, how can you solve problems if you don't empathize with those experiencing the problem? When we argue "I can't imagine what it is like to be...," we are actually stating that we will only sympathize with those experiencing the problem and have no desire to truly understand. If we don't understand the issue as leaders, how can we assist in solving the problem? In essence, we leave it to those experiencing the problem to develop the solution, and that is not leadership.

In any leader, all of the aforementioned qualities—loyalty, humility, curiosity, and empathy—can only be had with a strong dose of self-awareness and self-control. Of his father in later years, Aurelius observed:

> *"What is recorded of Socrates was no less applicable to him, that he had the ability to allow or deny himself indulgences which most people are as much incapacitated by their weakness from refusing as by their excesses from appreciating. To be thus strong enough to refrain or consent at will argues a consummate and indomitable soul—as Maximus also demonstrated on his sick-bed."*

For anyone to lead effectively, all of these qualities must be had, but it takes a certain strength of character—which also must be cultivated—in order to employ them. If we truly focus on these four traits, leadership is a forgone conclusion – if we miss any of these traits, we are destined to be mediocre at leadership, at best. The cultivation of these traits, as they have been for thousands of years, are the keys to great leadership.

If one is looking to dominate and control others, one is not a leader;
Leaders exist to allow others to reach their individual capacity.

XXIII. LEAD BY EXAMPLE

"I don't have to go up to the guys and tell them to hustle.

They see the way I play.

Leadership comes by example."

・*Willie Stargell*・

"Lead by example," it commonly professed. But how does this actually function in practice?

Here's a secret. *There is no such thing.*

Consider a simplistic but popular example of a scenario where the phrase is commonly utilized: an underage party where there is alcohol present. Young adults are often encouraged to eschew drinking while "setting the example" for their peers. How effective of a leadership strategy is this?

Imagine two students at the party wishing to lead. Both popular, intelligent, hardworking, and admired, neither one chooses to drink. The first decides that he is going to lead by example, so he stands prominently in the center of the room, where all can see him clearly not drinking. When offered a drink, he states loudly, "No! I am not drinking! This is wrong!" He even gives disapproving looks at others who walk by with alcohol.

A second student does much the same thing. However, once having taken the center of the room, clearly not drinking, she calls for the attention of the party. Explaining to them that she is not drinking because she thinks it is wrong, she calls upon them to join her and not drink either. Providing a clear argument for her case, she suggests to the group that they join her in throwing out their drinks and getting some soda.

While both students have admirable objectives, there is still a massive difference between the two. The young man did not lead; he only set the example. His action was passive, and to lead is an action. To lead, there must be a declarative; something along the lines of "follow me," or "do what I do." While he certainly set the right example, his actions were not necessarily enough to inspire the actions of others—possibly because no one even recognized that they were supposed to look to him for leadership. Despite his popularity and capability to lead, reputation and status do not automatically imply leadership; the only thing that implies leadership is assuming the role of leader by making a call to action. "I'm not drinking—*who's with me*?" This is what the second leader did, bravely standing out from the crowd not just with her actions, but by declaring herself a situational leader and giving specific guidance on what she wanted to have happen.

When you believe that it is enough to just "lead by example," no one knows that they are supposed to follow you. They don't know your vision, and they don't get any guidance. They don't even know that you are the one they are to be looking to for leadership. While the example above may seem sophomoric, it is not far off from larger issues that we commonly deal with as a country today. Would we want young people idly standing by as a peer was being bullied "leading by example" by not bullying? Or would we want them to set the example and lead by saying "stop," and physically intervening if necessary? On an international level, our country does this every day when we become engaged in the affairs of other nations, protecting human rights that are not being defended. Do we stay home and "lead by example?" Or do we set the example and lead by intervening in the name of the innocent?

This is far from simply a matter of semantics. True leadership is about other people, and leading by example refutes that principle. We call it "leading by example," but what it really looks like is taking care of yourself and doing the right thing—but not really doing anything to actually make others better. In this sense, the very notion of leadership by example is deeply egocentric, in that it presupposes others would look to you for leadership *sua sponte* (of their own accord). What makes you so special that just because you are doing the right thing, others would wish to follow suit?

So, you can set the example – a fine and honorable endeavor, to be sure, but questionable in its effectiveness—or you can set the example...and lead.

There is no such thing as leadership by example.
You either set the example, or you set the example—and
lead.

XXIV. DELEGATION

"Here lies a man who knew how to enlist the service

of better men than himself."

· *Andrew Carnegie* ·

In 1901, Andrew Carnegie delivered a speech at the Stevens Institute of Technology in Hoboken, New Jersey. That day, he stated his wish to have the above sentiment inscribed on his tombstone—that he had been nothing more than "a man who knew how to enlist the service of better men than himself." That is a humble request from a man whose legacies of industrialism and philanthropy stand strong over a century later. But this thought is not just emblematic of Carnegie's humility. It speaks also to an essential truth of success: beyond a certain scale, success is entirely contingent upon an individual's ability to delegate.

Of course, we know this. A chef cannot stir four pots at once—although the chef may want to. This is the paradox of delegation: although it is necessary, we rarely want to do it. To delegate means to renounce control, and that makes us uncomfortable. It requires finding people we trust and tasking them to oversee matters for us—serving as the chef's third and fourth hands, if you will.

Leaders often struggle with this, saying, "I can do it better;" "It is easier if I do it;" "It will be done faster if I just handle it." They may even be right. So, why delegate, then?

It is a delicate balance when we delegate. The purpose of delegation is for the leader to give away tasks in order to free up more personal bandwidth. A leader who remains overly involved in delegated tasks has only complicated matters, as now they have increased their workload by introducing the delegated individual as a force of entropy and source of uncertainty. Conversely, the leader who does not remain involved enough in delegated tasks runs the risk of affairs spinning out of control. A balance must be struck, and it is a fine and nuanced line to walk.

We frequently push others to operate outside of their "comfort zones," explaining to them that this is how we grow and develop. We need to follow this advice when we think about delegation, as well. How do we know how much to delegate? Here is a rule of thumb: if we are not uncomfortable with the amount of work we have given away, we have not delegated enough. Eventually, we will cross a threshold where we begin to feel just slightly uncomfortable with the amount of work we have entrusted to others. At that point, we have struck the right balance. This is where our teams and businesses can grow most efficiently. When delegating, as yourself: how comfortable am I?

When you just begin to feel uncomfortable,
You have given up the right amount of control.

XXV. COLLABORATION

"The Secretary of War is hereby authorized and directed to issue

a citation in the name of the President of the United States,

as public evidence of deserved honor and distinction,

to any organization, unit, detachment, or installation

of the Army of the United States..."

‧Executive Order 9075, signed by Franklin D. Roosevelt‧

The Presidential Unit Citation and Meritorious Unit Award...of the military awards and honors prominently displayed on servicemembers' uniforms, these are worn set apart from the others on the opposite side of the chest. This is for a distinct reason: while most of the awards are indicative of individual achievement, a unit citation honors not just the performance of one, but of the whole.

Some of the greatest achievements in United States military history have merited the awarding of this honor. Consider the storied First Marine Division in the Korean war, who received the Presidential Unit Citation for their actions in 1951. Their award citation, in part, reads:

"For extraordinary heroism in action against enemy aggressor forces in Korea...Spearheading the first counteroffensive in the spring of 1951, the FIRST Marine Division, Reinforced, engaged the enemy in the mountainous center of Korea in a brilliant series of actions unparalleled in the history of the Marine Corps, destroying and routing hostile forces with an unrelenting drive ...The outstanding courage, resourcefulness and aggressive fighting spirit of the officers and men of the FIRST Marine Division, Reinforced, reflect the highest credit upon themselves and the United States Naval Service."

This citation refers to the collective efforts of over 22,000 Marines, by the way, who comprised the 1st Marine Division in Korea. No small force by any measure—and it took a force of this size to achieve such towering feats. The combined commitment of individuals in collaboration, each bringing their A-game to the table; that's the only thing that enabled such a large-scale accomplishment.

It makes sense in a military context, doesn't it? Of course, no one man or woman—even a Marine, who might tell you otherwise—could win a war single-handedly. These things are accomplished on a far grander scale. Every military success our nation has ever achieved has resulted from the joint efforts of multiple branches, services, and units. Unit citations were devised to honor these feats, and to acknowledge the combined efforts of many which led to a far greater outcome than any individual could have ever achieved on their own.

Imagine if we prioritized collaboration in schools the way that we do in the military. What might a child's report card look like? "Mrs. Johnson's eighth grade homeroom is awarded an A for their collective work in Social Studies this school year. The students collaboratively researched, studied, and presented a group project on U.S. history the likes of which this middle school has never seen." It almost seems absurd to us, doesn't it? Perhaps at first it seems to be a silly example. But pause and read it again.

What was your gut reaction this time? A project on U.S. history—no one would object to that. But awarding everyone the same grade—isn't that a cop out? How are we supposed to know who really excelled and who was just dead weight? Without competitively ranking the students' achievements in some way, how are we to identify the cream of the crop? Isn't that in part what school is for, after all? Identifying the "best" so that we can funnel them off to the "best" colleges and the "best" careers?

Herein lies a radical notion. Much of what we will be asked to do in our adult lives will be reliant, above all, upon our ability to collaborate and contribute, alongside others, to a collective endeavor. The Amish, raising a barn in a day. A software company devising, implementing, and launching a new product. The team of doctors and nurses involved from start to finish in the process of a heart transplant. Running a household and raising a family alongside a partner or spouse. Bringing home the most wins in Super Bowl history. Viewed in this light, what in our adult lives is entirely *not* reliant upon collaboration? Barring the adventures of an individual survivalist in the wild, even the success of an athlete in an individual sport such as tennis or alpine skiing is still reliant upon their interaction with an extensive team of coaches, trainers, and training partners. It really is impossible in this life to "go it alone."

Why, then, do we not prioritize the ability to collaborate as being one of the primary objectives towards which we aspire to educate ourselves and our children? In this case, it may above all be the result of complacency, habit, tradition, and "the way things have always been done." The Western educational system was originally founded upon the model of European monasteries, which sought to create uniformity and individual excellence. This needed to be the case, given that the primary objective of this training was to produce monks (and nuns) who could flawlessly copy manuscripts and teach the gospel from memory without the help of written texts, which were not always easily come by. The antiquated skillset is no longer needed today, but the means by which it was perpetuated persists throughout American academe.

Still, it needn't be. Our access to information is very different now. Our younger generations will never have to wait two weeks to track down a new library book unless they want to; everything can be found on their smartphones. As such, the educational model which eschews collaboration is quickly becoming obsolete. In fact, the ability for individuals to collaborate is precisely what we need to be focusing on. Looking ahead to the future, as more of human capabilities are integrated into cyber technologies, the human ability to collaborate will become one of our primary assets. We won't be needed for the easy jobs anymore, but our human ability to navigate nuanced social relationships enables us to collaborate on a level that even the most "intelligent" artificial intelligence cannot yet fathom. Collaboration, after all, is emotionally and psychologically complex. It requires us to empathize, cooperate, communicate, understand, and compromise. These aren't generally things that come naturally to computers.

We must, for this reason, give ourselves, and our teams, permission to collaborate. We need to look beyond to the academic model under which we were all trained and understand that, in our increasingly complex adult world, collaboration is the key to our survival and enduring relevance. We must stop just awarding individuals for achievement. We need to move towards rewarding teams for their combined accomplishments. If we want a future that works together it is not an option; it is essential.

A life focused on 'we' is infinitely richer than a life focused on 'me.'

XXVI. HOW TO HELP A TEAMMATE

"Be team people, whether in athletics, business, or a profession.

This is a personal discipline developed early in life.

Work with other people, support them, encourage them,

and they will support and encourage you."

· *Jerry Hoffberger* ·

"The way of a warrior is not to destroy and kill,

but to foster life, to continually create."

· *Morihei Ueshiba* ·

There is an immature presumption that commonly plagues individuals in leadership positions. It seems innocent and well-intentioned enough: we tend to believe that leading others means correcting them and telling them what adjustments to make.

We learn to coach others in this way—whether in the workplace, at home, on the battlefield, or in the arena of sport—because it is the earliest type of coaching to which we are exposed in our lives. Parents correct their children from the moment they are capable of understanding chastisement: say "please" and "thank you," set the table with the fork to the left of the plate and the knife and spoon to the right, here is how to tie a shoe, and so-forth. When children grow old enough to leave the home, this style of training continues, as the Western educational system is founded upon the presupposition that the student will submit work to the teacher to silently accept evaluation and correction.

There is nothing inherently wrong with this style of leadership. When it comes to being taught new skills, children are blank slates and frequently in need of explicit instruction. It is an effective means of imparting to them the skills that they will need to survive in a challenging and complex adult world.

But what happens when we grow into adults among our peers? When we are tasked with leading high performing teams? When we are not leaders by title at all, but rather teammates among other competent adults? Then how do we lead? Is this style still appropriate?

In the adult context, the leadership style under which we learned to perform as children and students (even at the collegiate level) rapidly becomes obsolete. What was to us as children and young adults valuable feedback starts to feel like bossiness and condescension between adults. It becomes unwelcome, and it creates interpersonal friction.

Failing to recognize this effect can become insidiously corrosive within teams. Consider the following example borrowed from real life coaching experience.

A big name second-year NFL receiver misses a catch in practice. The coach approaches him and offers some well-intentioned advice: "Here's how you need to hold your hands to make that catch." The player remains respectful, but a flash of aggravation comes over his eyes. He accepts the instruction, but doesn't really listen, and his reaction is puzzling. He is a professional athlete; part of his job involves being coached. Why would it bother him to receive coaching and instruction in his game?

Because he is a grown man who has earned a solid reputation in the NFL for a reason. In his lifetime, he's completed thousands—if not tens of thousands—of similar catches. Football is his craft and his life's work. He *knows* how to catch a football. There is obviously another reason why he missed the catch.

The coach means well, but his coaching style has been so conditioned by our culture of teaching by critique and correction that he fails to hone in on this difference. The receiver is not a young person learning to catch a football for the first time; he is a professional athlete. By failing to acknowledge his player's baseline level of competency, the coach misses the opportunity to have productive interaction and actually solve the problem at hand.

What if the coach had found a way to respond to his player while acknowledging his player's competency and self-awareness? The encounter may have gone something like this. Player misses catch. Coach approaches. "Hey. What happened there? Why did you miss that ball?" Player responds: "You know what, coach? I was so busy worrying about the safety that was coming up above me

- 136 -

that I didn't see what was happening. I missed the ball because I got my head around too slow!"

In this case, no "coaching" is required, and practice can resume. The player is on top of it, and aware of what needs correcting. The coach understands what the player is struggling with, so he can observe the particulars of that dynamic from the sideline. It's an efficient adaptation to rapidly correct the problem.

In this context, the coach is functioning more as a facilitator than a teacher – and herein lies the difference between coaching and leading; coaching instructs, while leadership develops. Instruction tends to be a one-way conversation, while development is a conversation with question and feedback, where both participants are fully engaged. The player is, in all likelihood, a better receiver than the coach himself. The coach's job is to help his player fine-tune his craft and broaden his player's big-picture awareness. It's a subtle, nuanced, mature, efficient, and productive approach to the problem.

Of course, if the coach says, "Hey, what happened there?" and the player isn't sure, the coach's job expands into helping the player figure out what actually happened. Perhaps the player needs more time to think, or maybe he wants to review some video; whatever might help the player gain necessary insight, the coach's duty is to facilitate that.

The coach's job, in short, is not to create players; it is to develop them, and there is a difference.

The same is true for anyone attempting to coach or lead other competent individuals who are beyond the initial learning stage. This is how peers can lead each other, as well. It is just as easy to ask a peer or coworker, "Hey, what happened there?" as it is to inundate them with your unsolicited (and likely unwelcome) two cents. Honoring your team's competency is a sign of respect, and in doing so, you are also fostering their self-awareness and ability to self-correct: both hallmarks of personal development.

The principle is this: When you see something go wrong, let your first instinct be to listen before you talk. Be curious before knowing. This is how teamwork is fostered, and how a team can elevate itself from within.

Be curious before knowing.

XXVII. GUIDANCE AND 100%

"Individual commitment to a group effort:
that is what makes a team work, a company work,
a society work, a civilization work."
· *Vince Lombardi* ·

"And the strength of the pack is the wolf
And the strength of the wolf is the pack."
· *Sir Rudyard Kipling* ·

There is nothing quite so demeaning as being asked to
perform a simple task, only to be watched over our
shoulder the entire time. It's a universally loathed
leadership style, yet it's so common that one wonders if
most leaders are even aware when they are doing it:
micromanaging.

Why do we hate this so much? Human beings enjoy
autonomy, for one thing. On another much deeper level,
we can't stand to be micromanaged because it is reflective
of the presupposition of our incompetence, a lack of trust
in who we are and what we can do. Overbearing oversight
subliminally tells us, "I don't believe in you; you will
screw this up if I don't monitor your every move."
Perhaps, in a worst-case scenario, it can even evoke a
passive-aggressive response that results in the exact
opposite outcome than that which the micromanager

hoped to elicit. It is, in short, demoralizing and demotivating.

The negative outcomes often brought about by micromanaging prove a broader and much more valuable principle of leadership: people will give you what you expect of them. If you expect someone to fail, be prepared for them to meet your expectation. But if you expect your people to succeed beyond your wildest dreams—and they know how much you believe in their potential—be prepared to watch them soar.

This doesn't mean that your people won't need guidance. Of course, they will. But autonomy and guidance are not mutually exclusive. Consider the example of the leader who has chosen to delegate to the team a particularly challenging task. "Go work on it, and come back with a 30% solution," the leader might ask, before handing everything over to the team. When the team comes back with that 30%, the leader can pause to assess their direction. Are they on the right track? If so, it's back to work with a "come back when you can show me the 50% solution," and so forth, right on up until they hit 100%. The leader leads by guiding the team's autonomy, checking in on their progress like looking for blazes painted on the trees lining a hiking trail. If the team goes astray? Guide them back to the path, and then let them continue on their own until they reach their goal.

The key to developing your people is to guide them through this type of iterative process while ensuring that their efforts are continuously evaluated and refined. The goal is constant improvement until a satisfactory goal is reached, and under ideal circumstances, with each iteration a team will grow increasingly invested in their efforts. As their leader, the objective is to maintain absolute and unwavering faith that they will achieve their goal while intermittently coaching them through this cyclical iterative process of trying and refining.

[not slipping

Many leaders believe that this is unnecessary, and they provide minimal to zero guidance while trusting and assuming that their people will just "get it" immediately. The problem with this approach is that, while the people may give 100% effort to the project and return to their leader with great pride in their accomplishments, their sense of pride will quickly be dashed if they discover that they have directed their efforts in entirely the wrong direction. Any criticism to their work, regardless of how constructive, is still criticism, and in one way or another, it is going to be a blow to them—especially when they are proud of their work and have invested a great deal of time and energy into the project. They will walk away frustrated at having to start over. So much work accomplished and so much effort expended, only to be redone. The cost of such a misstep is not to your outcome, or even to your time; it is to your leadership and to the development of your people.

This is not the easiest nor the least labor-intensive form of leadership. It may not be the most efficient, either. But, more than any other style, this method will help the team members develop their individual confidence and capabilities. If a team leader dictates an entire project down to the most minimal detail and assigns every task, the project may get done well, but how much more experience will the team members have really gained?

How much will they have they grown? How much will they have developed themselves and become greater assets to their team—and to their leader—than they were before they started?

Through the iterative process of coaching your team to their 100% solution, you will find that your team will grow in competence, motivation, and self-confidence. It is the key to developing your people.

What an iterative process in development lacks in efficiency,
It creates in competency.

XXVIII. HUNT THE GOOD

"The key is to keep company only with people who uplift you;

whose presence calls forth your best."

• *Epictetus* •

What's the difference between being "led" and being "managed?"

Think about it. You were probably managed at your first retail job. Your manager's sole responsibility, as far as you were concerned, was to ensure that you were following all procedures, identifying the instances when you stepped out of line, and ensuring your future compliance.

It is often simply stated, "You manage things, and you lead people." But it is certainly much deeper than that.

Managing is functional in this type of transaction. The employee signs on to provide a service, their duties remain relatively static from day today, and the manager cracks the whip when they step out of line. Though never ideal, it's common practice, and it works well enough in low level situations. The employee's loyalty to the company and their motivations for working aren't important; the only imperative is that the employee shows up on time and completes the tasks he or she was hired to do.

But management and leadership are two different things. In higher level situations where uncertainty abounds and agility is required, management is no longer an effective leadership style. Management doesn't breed loyalty, motivation, or inspiration; on its dictatorial path to ensuring compliance, it kills them all.

The fundamental problem with management is that its sole purpose is to hunt the negative—seek out what's done incorrectly, and discipline the employee for it. Think about that—management doesn't look to solve deeply rooted problems and their causes; instead, it looks to identify faults (s), discipline the responsible parties, and make sure that the fault never happens again. It doesn't look to develop people; it looks to "fix" them – and when fixing anything, you have to look at what is broken first. Find what is wrong, and then make it right.

True leadership is the complete opposite. Its objective?

To hunt the good.

Leadership isn't about "fixing" people; it is about developing them and assisting them in becoming their best selves. To accomplish development, you don't find what is wrong; you find what is *right*—and then build from that point. "To develop" derives from Old French and English terms for unwrapping and unfurling; it implies taking what is already there, and then helping it flourish to its full potential. When you focus on leadership in the form of developing your people, hunting the good is imperative, because the good is the starting point from which development begins. This works whether you are teaching kindergarten or leading an elite group of Special Operations warriors—hunting the good is what gets everybody to the next level. When you just look for what is wrong, you can only get to good, or what is expected, by fixing what is wrong. When you hunt for the good, you are elevating your people—and the entire organization.

Hunting the good isn't about painting a "rosy picture" and ignoring mistakes. Hunting the good is about first finding what is "right" with any given situation, and then allowing those you lead to identify issues and make recommendations for improvement. This is extremely difficult, and it goes against what most leaders have been trained to do their entire lives. Many leaders view their role as that of "solution developers," there to fix what is wrong and solve problems. However, leaders who take this approach find that their organizations are only as good as they are, not as good as they could be by harnessing all their people.

For example, consider a Commander that goes to the range to observe his Soldiers train marksmanship. The minute he arrives at the range, he can immediately identify ten things that are "wrong" with the training, another five things that could be done more effectively, and probably one or two more things that are just his own pet peeves. Seeing this, most Commanders would immediately go into "fix it" mode – calling over young officers and noncommissioned officers, explaining the error of their ways, describing how to fix every detail, and generally correcting everything in sight. However, what they don't realize is that this "fixing" is alienating their command. Who wants a boss that finds what is wrong with everything you do, and then corrects if for you? It is the leadership rub: leaders have more experience and knowledge, so they are more likely to see what is wrong than what is right. They are then trained to make what is wrong right, so they do exactly as they believe they are expected. This leads to subordinates that dread their leader's presence, and do their best to hide mistakes.

Now, consider the same initial range scenario, but imagine that this time, instead of identifying what is wrong with the training (six errors, which the Commander sees immediately), the Commander hunts for what is right, hunting for the good in what he sees. He first corrects those issues that might cause the loss of life, limb, or eyesight, but other than that, he lets the rest alone for a moment and searches, instead, for what is good. Only then does he ask if there is anything that they might want to do differently. On their own, his people identify four of the six issues he had identified initially, with solutions, and how they are acting on those solutions. The Commander then must consider if the other two issues are worth bringing up now. Sometimes, waiting and discussing it later is better.

This may seem soft to many. If there is an issue—why not fix it immediately? No time to coddle feelings; we are talking about the military. The goal here is to produce the best end state possible, is it not? What do feelings have to do with any of this?

Think about it this way.

If you've ever attended a child's school conference, you already know what this looks like. The teacher begins with the child's strengths: "Your son has progressed so much this year with his mathematics. He is a good classroom helper and he plays well with others." All positive things; things that the student should keep doing. The teacher continues, "His next goal is to become a more proficient reader." This sets the parent's mental wheels spinning. What could their son do to progress at reading? The parent offers a suggestion: "Maybe his reading is progressing more slowly because we have not focused enough on spelling with him at home. Perhaps I could work more with him on his spelling and phonics over the summer." Just like that, the parent has self-scrutinized, problem solved, and become invested in the solution—all because the teacher began by hunting the good.

How would the dynamic of the conference have changed if the teacher had begun the conference by hunting the negative, sharing no positives and only the terse observation that "Your son is falling behind in reading?" How would this have altered the dynamic of the exchange? The parent would have likely become defensive, perhaps pointed fingers, and perhaps accused the teacher of falling short. It would not have been pretty. It would not have been productive. And it would not have built the necessary collaborative rapport between Jimmy's parent and teacher that would likely lead to an optimal outcome for the student.

One important distinction: what we are talking about here is not the commonly distained "crap sandwich," where we sandwich negative feedback with positives on both sides. This transparent and insincere tactic achieves little, and usually results in only negative feedback being remembered, anyway. What we are encouraging here, instead, is a true and sincere effort to identify and highlight the best in every situation—because in any situation, no matter how dire, there are always positives to be found. And when we allow others, sometimes even through directed facilitation, to identify their own areas for improvement, they will own the identification—and the ensuing solution.

The key to hunting the good is this. Identify what your people are doing right, and focus your feedback on what is going well. They will very often identify their own areas for growth. This isn't soft or an expression of weakness; rather, it is an effective way of ensuring that your people take the initiative to develop themselves beyond just your expectation. By hunting the good in every situation, we change our mindset and their accompanying reactions. We focus on positive, not by ignoring the negatives, but by acknowledging what is good, and allowing for self-discovery to solve for the less-than-optimal.

When we hunt the good, we move people forward.

XXIX. NOT PROACTIVE, NOT REACTIVE, JUST ACTIVE

"A good plan, violently executed now, is better than a perfect plan next week."

‧ *General George Patton* ‧

"Take time to deliberate,
but when the time for action has arrived,
stop thinking, and go."

‧ *Napoleon Bonaparte* ‧

In its earliest known usages, dating back to only 1933, the term "proactive" was used to express the opposite of "reactive." If "reactive" means acting behind the curve, "proactive" means acting beforehand. Proactive action anticipates an event and preemptively acts.

In many contexts, this is a positive thing. If I am proactive, I anticipate future challenges and act to mitigate them before they can become an issue. If I am heading out of town for two weeks, and I know that two bills will come due while I'm away, I pay them in advance to avoid an issue. Proactive action is anticipatory in nature, and on an individual level, there is no reason why it wouldn't be highly desirable.

On an organizational level, however, proactive action can become problematic because it entails a higher margin for error than actions that can be taken with greater levels of certainty. Because of this, when leaders ask our people to be "proactive," we must simultaneously ask ourselves if we are prepared and willing to deal with the fallout if these proactive choices miss the mark.

In Special Operations, we actually condition our people to be proactive. Across the board, the expectation is that our people find something to do and then do it; even if it is the wrong choice, they are doing something. A Private comes to the NCO and says, "Hey, this equipment was getting wet, so I moved it inside." His choice to move the equipment is a reaction to the rain; as such, the NCO comes back: "Well, why didn't you look at what the weather was going to do and move it before it even got a little bit wet?" The expectation in the world of Special Operations is that challenges are anticipated and handled before they have a chance to become issues.

Having not been specifically ordered to move the equipment, what if the Private had anticipated the rain and moved the equipment, but put it in the wrong place? From the NCO's perspective, this is still better than the previous scenario. In Special Operations, proactive is *always* preferable; mistakes are expected, accepted, and underwritten when they result from proactive choices.

The key to this approach, which bears reiteration? When proactive action is taken, mistakes are inevitable and—as such—they must be, as previously mentioned, "expected, accepted, and underwritten." The problem in business, leadership, and athletics, is that we often ask our people to be "proactive," but we remain intolerant of mistakes. In doing so, we actively de-incentivize our people from doing the exact thing we are asking for. The farther ahead of the anticipatory curve you act, the less certainty you have about your action, and the more you risk being incorrect or failing. People need to understand, when we ask them to be proactive, that we are good with this.

Of course, perhaps we are not good with this at all. For whatever reason—money, victory, Chain of Command, Board of Directors—it could be that we are in a position where we need to be more risk averse. In this scenario, we have to ask our people to be not proactive, not reactive, but *just active.* Doing the right thing, at the right time, for the right reason. In this scenario, we are looking to find that sweet spot for action. We are not anticipating the future, nor are we reacting to the past; we are interacting with the present in an active and conscientious way.

Innovation requires proacting;
Discipline requires acting;
Failure requires reacting.

XXX. DELIBERATE CULTURE

"Recognizing that I volunteered as a Ranger, fully knowing the hazards of my chosen profession, I will always endeavor to uphold the prestige, honor, and high esprit de corps of my Ranger Regiment."

• *The Ranger Creed* •

The opening line of the Ranger Creed: words that, over the years, have inspired thousands of men—and now a few women—to achieve more than they ever thought possible. This is the power of a deliberate culture: it sets a course, and challenges us to follow.

The Ranger Creed, the SEAL Ethos, the Special Forces Creed…these are not the same thing as a mission statement. Mission statements state objectives, and establish what an organization hopes to accomplish. Vision statements establish what it will take to get there. The ethos or creed, on the other hand, is a statement of culture. It establishes who you are as an organization, and who you will strive to be. The mission may be the source of the team's objectives, but it is the culture that determines how the team will reach them. Of course, it may need to be highly specific. As Robert Rogers—author of the 1789 "28 Rules of Ranging"—once famously advised, "You can lie all you please when you tell other folks about the Rangers, but don't never lie to a Ranger or officer."[18] Think about that. Rogers didn't just say, "Have integrity"; nor did he specifically say, "Always tell the truth." Rogers gave his people context of the value of honesty and how to apply it. This is both guiding and freeing at the same time.

In order to have a deliberate culture, leaders need to recognize that expectations must be understood by everyone on the team. If the CEO can describe the company culture, but the employees two doors down don't see it the same way, that is not a deliberate culture. This is because deliberate cultures are the result of integrated values in context. Simply stated, deliberate culture is the agreed upon values of a collective group and how they will be applied in that group. Where deliberate cultures do not exist, they can easily be born with a little prompting. All it takes is to simply ask your people: "Who do you want to be?" Leaders are often surprised to discover that the answer they receive is exactly what the leaders themselves would say. One lacrosse team took this question, evolved it into a deliberate statement of culture, and went on to win a Big 10 championship—taking their season farther than they had in years. The most truthful and enduring statements of culture are not dictated from the top down; they are born of the very people whom they are designed to guide.

---

[18] Robert Rogers, "Robert Rogers' Standing Orders," GoArmy.com. Accessed 12/3/18.
https://www.goarmy.com/ranger/about-the-rangers/rodgers-orders.html

Mission statements came to business in the 1940s, most likely due to a population coming out of wartime military service. Vision statements started to appear shortly thereafter in the 1950s. Both had a tremendous impact on business, as mission statements outlined what organizations did, while vision statements put forth where they were going and how they planned to get there. Still, neither of these documents addressed the "who" that makes up the organization, nor the type of discipline required of both leaders and employees. Ultimately, though, what organizations want—and need—is for people to the right thing, at the right time, for the right reason. This needs to be internalized before people can act (not react) on the fly, in unpredictable circumstances, coming to solutions independently while meeting the intent of the organization and its leaders. This paradigm shift allows leaders to go beyond just policies, procedures, and metrics. Leaders need something that provides principles on how to lead, and the solution is a culture statement that tells all members of the organization who they are.

How powerful can culture be? A memory from 3rd Ranger Battalion as a young lieutenant. It was Friday morning officer PT, and before every session they would say the Ranger Creed to focus themselves for their training. At the same time, the clock struck 0600—the time on every base when a cannon goes off and the flag goes up, to stay up until evening. No matter where they are and what they are doing, all soldiers on base turn to face that flag and salute. Still, only when this team of officers had finished the Ranger Creed did they turn to salute the flag. This is how powerful a culture can be.

Though every collective group has a culture, most are not deliberate. The rules are imagined in each individual's head, and applied as they are understood. Sometimes this works, and organizations can be successful. However, without a deliberate culture, we are asking our people to "play without a rulebook," setting them (and our organization) up for failure. A deliberate culture provides a set of principles and agreed upon values for the group and puts them in context so they can be applied appropriately for that organization—and its people's—success

You cannot successfully determine what you should do,
and how you should do it,
until you know who you are.

ELECTISSIMI

(Elite)

XXXI. EARN IT EVERY DAY

"That which Fortune has not given, she cannot take away."

• Seneca •

"At dawn, when you have trouble getting out of bed, tell yourself,

'I have to go to work—as a human being. What do I have to complain of,

if I'm going to do what I was born for—the things that I was brought into the

world to do? Or is this what I was created for?

To huddle under the blankets and stay warm?'"

• Marcus Aurelius •

"It had long since come to my attention that people of accomplishment

rarely sat back and let things happen to them.

They went out and happened to things."

• Elinor Smith •

Many people think of goal-setting like climbing a mountain: focus on getting to the top; put in the time, with dedication and singularity of focus, until that objective is achieved. Whether that goal is earning a spot in a Special Operations Unit, winning the Super Bowl, graduating from a top medical school, or scoring that C-level position at a Fortune 500 company, there comes a time in many people's lives where their highest goal is achieved. They make it to the top.

What happens when a climber makes it to the top of Everest? They don't have much time to waste. They take a few pictures and hang out on the summit before their retreat, carefully timing their descent to avoid the pitfalls and dangers brought on by nightfall and incoming weather. But when we reach a great personal or professional goal, the pinnacle of our success, we plan to stay at the top indefinitely. No one ever plans to take steps backwards. When we achieve success, we wish to hang onto it for as long as possible. More like building a house on the summit of Everest and moving in.

The problem is that real life doesn't work in either of these ways. When it comes to the type of success that is earned, there's only one way to hang onto it, and that's to earn it again. And again. Every. Single. Day.

What does that mean, exactly?

It means that whatever your role in life—however you define your own personal "pinnacle of success,"—you first need to get there. And then you have to keep climbing. There is no room for complacency, ego, or resting on your laurels. You have work to do, and people depending on you. Your focus cannot be just on maintaining your success; you have to stay open, innovative, and focused. Every day, you must again earn your right to have that role. It's like climbing up the down escalator: in order to stay at the top, you have to keep moving. Otherwise, you'll be swept straight back down to where you came from, and others will pass you by.

Why think of it in these terms? Because any high performing team or company that falls victim to complacency may be good, but it will never be great. Greatness is only achieved with a singularity of focus that allows the boundary of what is possible is stretched towards that which is merely imagined. You can't make the imaginary into reality without innovation, drive, and dedication: the same qualities that set individuals apart to begin with and drive them to the top are the very qualities that make the "impossible" possible. The qualities that make what is "good" into what is "better"—put into practice every single day.

When you are a member of a high performing team or organization, your position there is a privilege—not a right. Understanding this, with humility and gratitude, you can approach your role with a renewed sense of vigor and dedication. You are a critical part of an interdependent group making up your team or organization, and seeing your role in this light, it becomes natural to want to uplift everyone around you as well as yourself. You become invested. The concern has to shift from: "I don't want to let them down," to: "How can I bring everyone up?"

The Ancient Greeks understood the beauty and purpose of a human being aspiring to their highest potential; this is why they embraced the concept of areté. It doesn't matter how much purpose one derives from the organization for which he currently works—what matters more to a person of areté is that he is highly effective (good at what he/she does), self-actualized (knows and understands him or her self), and committed to forging within himself the highest potentialities of which humans are capable (a desire to improve). This—aspiring to greatness for its own sake— can be achieved in any context. And, because many of our life's activities are carried out in groups or on teams (rather than individually), it makes sense that we should remain humbly committed to not only self-improvement, but also to constantly finding ways to elevate the others upon whom our own success also depends. This concept creates a thought process that expands our good work beyond that of ourselves and our families, and allows this philanthropic ideal to expand to our work and our communities.

There's a secret to the way that elite top performers think, and it's such an innate part of who they are that they rarely think to share it. This secret is in how they view each challenge—each "mountain" that they have to climb. While, for most people, the summit of the mountain is a finite point representing a goal that is reached, the elite performer looks at it differently. For the elite performer, the mountain has no summit. Each goal that they reach is merely a waypoint; a place to perhaps stop and take in the view, but also from which to refocus their vision on the next higher goal that once seemed out of reach. Because of this tendency—to constantly seek new challenges and perpetually strive for self-betterment—the concept of "earning it every day" is intrinsic to the elite performer's mindset.

To many of us, this may sound exhausting. We may ask ourselves where and when, if ever, such high performers would find peace.

The answer is that pace for the high performer comes from "measuring backwards." They look to see where they came from, appreciate how far they have come, and learn from their failures before re-orienting on the next goal. Their peace is not devoid of movement. Peace does not always require stillness; there can be peace found in the movement itself. Peace found as one progresses through learning and development. The goal may be the destination, but the peace for the high performer can be in the journey itself.

For the elite performer, life is a perpetual cycle of setting goals, striving towards them, achieving them, and then—with new perspective—setting the next goal, and the next one after that. Every day working, every day striving, and every day earning it all over again.

Growth only happens with movement.

XXXII. THE BEST VS. THE BEST AVAILABLE

"Ill fortune is of more use to men than good fortune...

The one deceives; the other teaches."

• *Boethius* •

The elite Special Operations Team had been grinding relentlessly, night after night, in pursuit of High Value Targets. Every night, they went out into the darkness, moving with incredible stealth and speed in relentless pursuit of their enemy. These were a conglomeration of the best warriors the United States had ever produced. Still, no matter what they tried, they continued to come upon "dry holes"—the HVTs they sought weren't there. They came down hard on themselves; it felt as if they were failing. To them, they were failing—and they never failed. They were the best in the world...or were they? Had they been surpassed, or were they losing their edge?

Aware of this feeling among his men, the Commander of this special unit stepped in. He gathered together all of his elements present to offer his guidance and perspective. The advice that he offered was unconventional and unexpected:

"Ok, you guys," he said, "Listen. You're not the best. You're the best available."

A humbling statement, in theory. Not the best? The Commander was speaking to the most elite units of the most elite Special Operations Forces in the entire United States Military. Was it a chastisement? In every other narrative, these men were accustomed to being told that not only were they the best their country had to offer; they were the best in the *world*.

But there's a curse that comes with being told that you're the best. It is not pride; at least not at this level of high performance—these men are the antithesis of complacency, striving constantly for self-betterment. Neither is it a lack of humility – these men were the definition of quiet professionals, letting their performance speak for itself. So, what was the Commander getting at?

What the Commander's statement actually gave them wasn't a taste of humble pie; it was freedom that came in the form of the permission to make mistakes.

It was a reminder that they, too, were human.

Because while it is a remarkable accomplishment to rise through the ranks to the top of the most elite units, making it to that level does not guarantee that these men are unequivocally and objectively the best people who could possibly exist. What it really means is that they are the best of those who chose that path and achieved that level of success—the best of the men who wanted to attend selection, made it through selection, and the best of those who were fortunate to not have injury or another adverse life event intervene in their ability to press onward. There are still plenty of others walking the earth who most certainly have the capability and capacity to excel at that same level, but are busy working in other career fields, serving in other segments of the military, or in society at large.

So, if humility and complacency weren't the concern for the team, what was?

The toxic belief that the best can't fail.

In fact, the Commander's statement showed, not only can the best fail; the best *should* fail from time to time. Failure—in this case: failure to locate the HVTs—still provides valuable data. Finding a dry hole doesn't tell you where the bad guys are, but it does tell you where the bad guys are not. Even more importantly, in order to learn, everyone must fail. This is an essential part of the learning process. And even on an elite team mostly operating on a no-fail margin of error, learning is still an essential feature of the adaptability that ensures success. At this level of performance, innovation is critical—how do you stay the best in the world if you're not constantly keeping ahead of the competition? How do you keep ahead?

You innovate. What happens when you innovate? You experience failure. What happens when you fail? You learn. What happens when you learn? You get better. Not a bad outcome.

Innovation is the byproduct of learning, and learning is the byproduct of failure. It must necessarily be so. Excellence, for this reason, is the result of an evolutionary process; as Aristotle said, "We do not act rightly because we have virtue or excellence, but rather we have those because we have acted rightly."

The wisdom in this commander's statement—that the men of this elite unit were "not the best, but the best available"—was the permission that these high-achieving, self-driven warfighters needed in order to accept that to err is not only human; it is a necessary feature of the learning process in which one must engage in order to continue to excel. Some failures, when born of negligence, are not a good thing. But failures that are born of trying to do something with effort and not succeeding—such as hitting a dry hole—are merely opportunities to learn what doesn't work. That is a step forwards; not a step backwards.

Think about that for a moment. Failure isn't taking a step backwards; it is taking a step forward by moving ahead and learning. How should this knowledge change the way that you lead? The way that you live?

When you think of yourself as not "the best," but rather as "the best available," the pressure valve is released. Everyone is fallible—we all have our own Achilles' heel. Learning is how we better ourselves; excellence is the learned product of habit, as Aristotle said. Learning entails failure, and failure imparts wisdom. By accepting that we are only the best available, we give ourselves the space to fail and, thus, the space to learn.

What happens when we deny ourselves this space to learn? The results can be nothing less than tragic. Consider the example of the great warrior Ajax, second only in strength and bravery among the Greeks to his dearest friend Achilles. When Achilles was killed in battle, Ajax was prepared to assume the vacated position of Achilles as the greatest. However, failure at the final and most important task to honor his brother in arms was the great warrior Ajax' undoing. He fell into a fury from which he never recovered, ultimately taking his own life. The great poet Sophocles, himself a General and a warrior in his own right, told the story of Ajax in a tragic play, lending Ajax the lamenting words of a great man dejected at his perceived sense of failure. "With what face shall I appear before my father," he asks; "How will he find heart to look on me, stripped of my championship in war, that mighty crown of fame that once was his?"[19] One event, and the perspective that the best can't fail, destroyed his mindset—and he came unraveled.

The wisdom of this play lives on. Sometimes, knowing you are the "best" creates a belief that you cannot fail. The Greeks understood this critical paradox: to be great requires more moments that lack greatness than moments of being great.

---

[19] Sophocles, *Ajax*, Transl. R.C. Trevelyan (Cornell University Library: 2009). http://classics.mit.edu/Sophocles/ajax.html

When we free ourselves from having to be "the best,"
We liberate ourselves to be better.

XXXIII. OPPORTUNITY DOORS

"Being courageous requires no exceptional qualifications, no magic formula, no special combination of time, place, and circumstance. It is an opportunity that sooner or later is presented to us all."

·*John F. Kennedy*·

"Comparison is the thief of joy."

·*Theodore Roosevelt*·

"Privilege" has become a buzzword in this country, and such a hot button topic that it has become dangerous to touch it anymore. "Check your privilege" has become a popular phrase on college campuses, where the philosophical underpinnings of future social programming intending to do just that is devised. By those definitions, one could hardly imagine a more privileged American than John F. Kennedy—born into a socially elite white East-coast family steeped in traditions of business, politics, and philanthropy; schooled at Choate and Harvard, raised between Hyannis Port and Palm Beach— the blueprint for his life emblematizes the archetype of American white male privilege.

Still, we all know how his story met a tragic ending, similar to the ending met by so many others within the fabled Kennedy clan. The truth of the matter is that all the opportunity in the world does not ensure a charmed life. While Kennedy's path to the White House may, in some ways, have been paved in gold, his life is not one that many of us would choose for ourselves knowing the fullness of the story.

For each individual, the life path is different. The doors to our opportunities may come in different sizes. Educated where he was, coming from the places he did, with the connections that he had, JFK's opportunity doors were enormous. His "privilege," as we like to say, afforded him that. Still, what happens to the child growing up impoverished in Appalachia or inner-city Detroit, harboring Presidential dreams of his or her own? Should we see Kennedy's example as utterly discouraging—that the opportunity doors to the Presidency exist only for people like him? And what good does holding such a belief do us?

We all have the tendency to think in this way, focusing too much on the places where our own opportunity doors are small while perceiving others' to be so much bigger. Still, it doesn't matter how downtrodden any of us imagine ourselves to be: everybody gets doors. The only difference is that not everybody's door is the same size, and the size of our door isn't up to any of us.

Maybe one person would have completed Ranger school if it hadn't been 30 degrees and raining the whole time. Maybe another would have gotten better grades in college if they hadn't been paying their own way through school. Maybe a third would have had an easier time starting a new business with a trust fund to fall back on. We all spend time imagining how our lives may have been easier or more successful if we had been given someone else's opportunity doors, but what good does this habit do any of us? None. In fact, that comparative analysis can actually hinder your success.

Every minute that we spend worrying that someone else's opportunity door is bigger than ours is 60 seconds that we could have spent focused on how we are going to breach our own door. We spend too much time trying to make doors equal, but all of this time is wasted when what we really need to be doing is focusing on our own doors. Because here is the crux of the matter: just because someone has a big opportunity door does not mean that they are ever going to walk through it. For every hardworking scholarship student earning A's while struggling their way through Harvard on their own dime, there is a legacy student with all expenses paid, drinking away their future at the local bars (or vice versa).

In Ranger school, soldiers take turns leading patrols. In this temporary leadership position, you are in charge of your team, and you're going to be judged for it. The kicker is that these patrols are held during different periods of training, and the geographical location (and climate) of any soldier's turn at the helm is anyone's guess. Your teammate gets the easy day in Florida—70 degrees, sunny, everyone is happy. It's a lucky break, but there are no breaks for you when you have to lead the team island hopping through swampland in the pouring rain, on day 7 when everyone is tired and hungry. When you are focused on leading your team and passing the course, what good does it do you to ruminate on your teammate's good fortune from a week ago?

Opportunity doors are what we make of them, plain and simple. At some point, there is nothing left to do but stop complaining about the size of your door, bust it open, and then make the door bigger for others to come through in the future. Stop talking and start doing.

We never achieve our goals by watching others achieve theirs;
Focus on your door.

XXXIV. GREATNESS

"If a man knows not to which port he sails, no wind is favorable."

·*Seneca*·

Greatness. While we aspire to it and admire it when we think we see it in others, its nature is nearly impossible to pinpoint. We know it when we see it, but how are we to define it?

The truth about greatness is that it exists beyond any subjective measure. Each individual's definition of greatness is as unique as their own fingerprint, crafted by experiences and influences built through a lifetime. For some, greatness is defined in almost childlike absolutes: prima ballerina, rock star, astronaut, CEO, or President of the United States. For others, greatness may be the more commonly achievable 2.5 kids with a white picket fence and comfortable retirement.

What is consistent across the board, then, is not "greatness" in and of itself, but rather the means by which it is pursued and achieved. However one defines it, there is only one way to achieve it: with the singularity of focus with which a future Olympic gold medalist pursues that prize. Every breath, choice, decision, and task is devoted towards that goal. What is enough? When is it enough? This can only be determined by the goal itself—and by one's proximity to it at any given moment.

The great Stoic philosopher Seneca wrote, "If a man knows not to which port he sails, no wind is favorable." Every journey must have a destination, and the path to greatness is a journey. Where is the journey headed? Once the course is set, each action becomes clear. Every choice is another opportunity to make headway on reaching the destination.

What are the implications of this in leadership terms? While each leader is busy pursuing her own definition of greatness, she must never forget to consider "greatness" as it is defined by each of the people under her guidance. How can she help push each of them towards their own idea of greatness, while also helping them to navigate towards organizational goals and visions that benefit the team? And how can she help them to reach the highest level of greatness that their capacity allows? It is for the leader to understand this, and guide accordingly. Not everyone has the capacity to be the Olympic Gold Medalist, but an appropriately set benchmark for success can feel just as rewarding when it is achieved.

As individuals, we must each learn to identify greatness: not as it is defined for others, but how we define it for ourselves. Once we identify what our own greatness looks like, we can determine the process necessary to achieve it, and then strive for it with a singularity of focus. Greatness is achievable—for everyone.

Greatness in any endeavor requires a singularity of focus toward your outcome.

XXXV. THE CYCLE OF GREATNESS

*"It is important to push yourself further than you
think you can go,*

*each and every day—and that is what separates the
good from the great."*

· *Kerri Strug* ·

There is another distinction about greatness that, if we are
ever to achieve it, we must acknowledge. There is the
greatness that we achieve when we meet the measure of a
goal we set out for ourselves, previously discussed. But
there is also is the flash of brilliance; the briefly achieved
pinnacle that constitutes the moment of greatness. These
are not the same thing.

Moments of human greatness stand alone, and often
endure indefinitely in popular memory. Whether we are
the ones living them or not, when we are privileged to
witness these rare occasions, it lights a fire within us. It
feels as though we are catching a glimpse of something
beyond ourselves: some level of human capacity that
exceeds what we ever thought possible.

Children dream of living these moments. Adults, more
aware of their improbability, marvel at them. All of us are
moved by them on a deep human level. Watching others
break the limits of all we ever thought possible gives us
the precious gift of hope that we, too, could one day enjoy
such pinnacles.

Consider the performance of Eli Manning and David Tyree in the iconic "helmet catch" moment that occurred in the final moments of Super Bowl XLII, and led to the Giants' 17-14 upset victory over the Patriots. With under two minutes left on the clock, Manning broke free from the grasp of 3 Patriots defenders to launch a 32-yard pass to wide receiver Tyree, who leapt into the air and secured the ball with one hand against his helmet. This seemingly impossible gesture resulted in a complete pass, on what turned out to be the drive for the game winning touchdown. We recognize that this is more than luck—it is the result of individual efforts toward greatness combining and culminating to create an apex performance.

A similarly iconic moment came in the 1996 Olympic performance of gymnast Kerri Strug. The US team was neck and neck with Russia for the gold, and when it came time for Strug to make a second vault attempt, the US team's hopes for gold hung mathematically on her shoulders. Her coach, Bela Karolyi, later recalled the injured 19-year-old asking him, "Do we need this?" followed by his own plea: "Kerri, we need you to go one more time. We need you one more time for the gold. You can do it; you better do it."[20]

What followed was an iconic moment in the history of sports. The diminutive athlete limped to the end of the

---

[20] Rick Weinberg, "Kerri Strug Fights Off Pain, Helps U.S. Win Gold," ESPN.com. June 29, 2008. Accessed November 30, 2018. https://web.archive.org/web/20080629004458/http://sports.espn.go.com/espn/espn25/story?page=moments%2F51

runway to make her final vault attempt. She landed, hopped onto her good foot, saluted the judges—and collapsed to her knees, having to be escorted back to her team's bench. Her performance was more than enough: her vault scored a 9.712, guaranteeing the Americans a gold medal finish. Her coach later carried her to the podium in his arms, after which she was treated at the hospital for her injuries. Again, not luck, but the product of an individual focused on greatness.

The images of Strug's triumphant moments following this vault have remained for decades symbols of all that the Olympics stand for. The images, and the story, endure in the public imagination because they motivate and inspire us. They make us want to be better and achieve more. This is a good thing. Still, if it were easy to attain these moments of greatness, we would all enjoy them more regularly. And if they just sporadically occurred amongst the undeserving like lightning strikes, we wouldn't find them nearly as inspiring, because we would see them as merely "lucky" occurrences rather than the product of hard work and effort. The reality is that we intuitively understand something deeper about the moment of greatness. What we see in such events isn't just the elation of someone who has won the lottery. Rather, in them we witness the momentary capitulation of a life's work. A pinnacle that justifies years of blood, sweat, tears, sacrifice, hard work, failures, learning, and dedication.

The tear-jerking "Thank You, Mom" commercial campaign that Proctor & Gamble ran during the 2014 and 2018 winter games was successful because we all share this awareness. We know that when we see an athlete reach a pinnacle of greatness, the moment bears depth and weight extending far beyond the reaches of what we have just witnessed. These commercials appeal to that awareness, depicting the tiny victories and huge sacrifices that a family puts in to support an athlete on their path to Olympic victory. When we look at an Eli Manning, David Tyree, or Kerri Strug, we see a beautiful flash of achievement that tells us that we are watching the culmination of years of hard work and sacrifice. We all understand because we all have, to some lesser extent, been there. We feel it in our hearts. We hope that the sacrifices we make in our own lives—whether in service of our own dreams or in service of the dreams of those we love—will prove equally to have been so worthwhile.

When we are in touch with this feeling, we are in the right space to understand what it really takes to attain greatness. Greatness, by definition, is never permanent, and it is never static. It is a pinnacle—a moment in time. Greatness is always fleeting, and what was once great does not always stand the test of time. Even when greatness does endure, it only remains in relation to where it was at one point in history—this is why records will always be broken, amendments will always be made, and people will always continue chasing the next best thing. So, if we are to pursue those moments of greatness, what should the rest of our time look like?

To achieve moments of greatness, it is not enough to just do what we have always done. If we are to pursue greatness, we must first continually pursue our own evolution and self-development. How is this achieved? Through innovation. As we innovate, we try new things, adopting what works for us and what makes us stronger and better. In other words, some innovations lead to success—and when they do, we learn. We learn what works, and we continue to do it. Perhaps this will lead to more moments of greatness, or perhaps this will feed us back into the cycle of innovation. Either way, innovation, success, and learning go hand in hand.

THE CYCLE OF GREATNESS

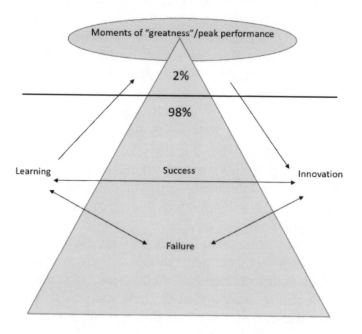

And what happens when our attempted innovations don't pan out, and we fail? Failure, too, leads to learning. It's how we learn what *doesn't* work, and this is equally important as knowing what *does*. What do we do when we fail? We learn, and then we try again: back to innovation, or "the drawing board," as they say. There are no losses; only wins and lessons.

How should this understanding affect our training? It is important for both leaders and their teams to recognize that, as much as we all desire those iconic moments of greatness in our own lives, the means of achieving them is not by seeking them. If we only seek out moments of greatness in practice and in competition, we fail to acknowledge that our focus actually needs to be on each of our own personal journey; not on being great. The journey, after all, is where we spend 98% of our time: innovating, succeeding or failing, and learning from it all. Greatness is just the pinnacle: that 2% moment of peak performance where the stars align for us. We can seek it, and make greatness our goal, but we must simultaneously acknowledge the paradoxical truth that we don't attain greatness by seeking it, but by putting in the work behind the scenes.

When it comes to greatness,
Apply the 2% / 98% rule:
To be great 2% of the time,
You must spend 98% of your time working to get there.

VADE
(Go Forth)

LIVE A LIFE OF PURPOSE

"The purpose of life is not to be happy.

It is to be useful, to be honorable, to be compassionate;

to have it make some difference that you have lived and lived well."

· *Ralph Waldo Emerson* ·

How do we live good lives? How do we do more than just "survive" from day to day? How do we feel like we are going in the right direction, and investing our efforts and energy worthily?

The purpose of life: it has been a primary question tackled by philosophers since the dawn of time. For some, life's purpose is contextualized by their religious beliefs. For others, there is no such philosophical catch-all. Either way, as Aristotle argued in the Ethics, there are universal, unlimited, real goods of the soul—goods that apply to all human beings, inexhaustible and unlimited in that it is impossible to have more of them than we need. For him, these goods are knowledge, skill, love, friendship, aesthetic enjoyment, self-esteem, and honor. We develop them through the practice of virtue, developing the good habits that ensure we choose things that are good for us and eschew those that harm us or hinder our happiness.

Even still, Aristotle understood another critical truth: action, in order to be defined as such, must be deliberately chosen. It must, in other words, be purposeful in nature. Most importantly, Aristotle says, we know the character of our acts by their purpose. He demonstrates this again and again in the Ethics[21] in discussions surrounding the topics of voluntary action and self-discipline (continence). The message is consistently the same: the purpose of an action is as important if not more important than the action itself.

Human beings have a short memory. Anyone who recalls having been a teenager and rejecting their parents' well-meaning guidance and advice with a "let me live my own life" knows that, for some inexplicable reason, it is in our nature to reinvent the wheel. We try our hand again and again at innovating theories of how to live the good life, and when we seek answers, we find contradictory messages. From one side comes "Get up and grind," "Get some," and "Sleep when you are dead," while in the other ear we hear "You have to stop and smell the roses," "Take some 'you' time," and—of course—"No one regrets the days they took off from work." So, which is it?

The dichotomy plagues and challenges us all, especially the high performers who are concerned with squeezing every drop of potential from both themselves and their

---

[21] Cf. Ethics VII.10 for Aristotle's discussion of incontinence: "And he acts willingly (for he acts in a sense with knowledge bothof what he does and of the end to which he does it), but is not wicked, since his purpose is good…and he is not a criminal; for he does not act of malice aforethought." Aristotle, *Ethics*, Transl. W.D. Ross. Accessed 11/8/18. **http://classics.mit.edu/Aristotle/nicomachaen.html.**

time on this earth. What should be our focus? We are encouraged "not to work so hard" and to "enjoy life," while simultaneously being told to "grind" and "relentlessly pursue our dreams." What we are left with is a feeling of confusion, shame, and guilt—either for not working hard enough, or for working too hard. What is right? What do we need to do? Again, we find ourselves feeling like the most ancient question of all still remains, for us, unanswered: what is the right way to live a good life?

For Aristotle, the solution to this dichotomy was "the golden mean," i.e. an ethical virtue that exists as an intermediate condition between extremes of excess and deficiency. Contemporary Americans, however, don't tend to think in this way. We are far too individualistic to accept absolutist advice. The truth is that there is indeed a golden mean in all things, but the golden mean doesn't look the same for everyone. The Greek men about and for whom Aristotle primarily wrote constituted a far more homogenous demographic than even your average NFL starting lineup, let alone contemporary, international, globalized society as a whole.

Today, when speaking universally about what it means to "live a good life," we have to consider just how different we all are. Different needs, different wants, different requirements at different times of life. To think that any single motivational message on a bumper sticker could speak to one and all is reductive, and probably downright impossible. In the midst of all this contemporary motivational background noise, it is easy to forget what the ancients knew well: life wasn't just defined by suffering, nor was it only about pure enjoyment. It was about purpose. When it comes down to it, the answer—for us all—is simple: to live a good life is to live a life with meaning.

A life with *purpose.*

The trick to living a good life is in finding that critical nexus where what you like to do intersects with that which you are capable of contributing to improve the lives of others, or the world at large. This is not about "finding your passion" or "identifying what brings you fire;" it is about identifying that thing you love to do that you can bring and offer up to the world as a gift to humanity. It is about deriving pleasure from what you do, while ensuring that you create a positive impact on the world around you. It is about the satisfaction that one derives from appreciating their own individual impact on the world. And it is about making a positive contribution: while some leaders may create things—ideas, objects, causes, processes—that make other things obsolete, their focus is always on creating the new. True leaders never set out to destroy; they aim only to create. It is a matter, above all, of perspective.

This doesn't mean that you may never need to take a breather and get reoriented with your purpose, taking some time (or a vacation) to ensure you are still connected to "who you are." We all lose our way sometimes, and this isn't a flaw; it's just life. Sometimes, it's important to get our bearings and ensure that we are still living as we intended. This doesn't necessarily require a trip to Nepal or living a van for a year of Eat-Pray-Love-type self-discovery. Often all it takes is pausing and lifting our head to survey our location in life. Life, after all, doesn't stop when you reorient—with everything you do, you are making your life and living your story. Taking time off doesn't stop time; time always moves forward. If life doesn't allow you to pause and reassess, review your life in stride. As you live it—*in medias res.*

When you do pause to reflect, use that precious time to focus not on how much or little you are working. Focus instead on what your purpose is, and how it can benefit the world. Remember our discussion of motivation vs. inspiration. When we polarize our thoughts and focus exclusively on either "the grind" or "the bliss," we live a motivated life. But when we live to purposefully impact the world, we live inspired lives of hope and trust: hope that what we are doing is worth it, and trust that we can do it. This is, in essence, living the inspired life. Living a motivated life is not only short-lived; it is ego-centric. A motivated life is a self-focused life; even if we do good, if it is about us and not purely for good's sake, it really is less impactful.

So, what is a good life? A purposeful life. An inspired life. A life not swayed by external motivators; not belittled or shamed by others' views of success; not self-centered in its frame of reference.

And how to achieve it? Identify what is yours to contribute, and find where it can be impactful: your purpose is thereby defined. Live for the betterment of others, but do it your way. In broadest terms: do it your way, but live a life of action.
Live to make the world a better place.

Living a motivated but self-serving life is nothing.
Living an inspired life of purpose is everything.

BIBLIOGRAPHIA

Aristotle. *Ethics.* Transl. W.D. Ross. Accessed 11/8/18. http://classics.mit.edu/Aristotle/nicomachaen.html.

---. *Metaphysics.* Transl. Hugh Lawson Trancred (Penguin: 1999).

Atalanta, Alice. "When Lightning Strikes Twice: What a World-Class Boxing Coach Father and His Green Beret Son Can Teach Us About the Nature—and Nurture—of High Performance." Havok Journal. 10/18/18. Accessed 12/6/18. https://havokjournal.com/culture/when-lightning-strikes-twice/

Aurelius, Marcus. *Meditations.* Transl. Maxwell Staniforth (Penguin: 2005).

Bracevich. Andrew. *Breach of Trust: How Americans Failed Their Soldiers and Their Country* (Picador: 2013).

DIRECTV. "Exclusive Pre-Fight Interview: Mayweather." Filmed 4/2013. YouTube video, 3:00. Posted 4/2013.https://www.bing.com/videos/search?q=exclusiv e+prefight+interview+mayweather&view=detail&mid =03B21139B04287DB44FD03B21139B04287DB44FD &FORM=VIRE.

A

Doerries, Brian. *Theater of War* (Vintage, 2016).

Douglass, Frederick. *The Essential Frederick Douglass.* Transl. Nicholas Buccola (Hackett, 2016).

Forni, P.M. *Choosing Civility: The Twenty-five Rules of Considerate Conduct* (St. Martin's Griffin: 2003).

Glick, JC and Sarah Ngu. *A Light in the Darkness: Leadership Development for the Unknown* (Lightning Press: 2017).

Hobbs, Angela. "Honor, Courage, Thumos, and Plato's Idea of Greek Manliness." *The Art of Manliness*. Podcast audio, 12/5/16.

Horace. "Ars Poetica." In *The Norton Anthology of Theory and Criticism*. Ed. Vincent B. Leitch (Norton: 2001).

Jenness, Kirik. "Cowboy Removed Hard Sparring From Training." Mixedmartialarts.com. 8/31/16. Accessed 12/3/18. https://www.mixedmartialarts.com/news/cowboy-removed-hard-sparring-from-training.

B

King, Jr., Martin Luther. *A Testament of Hope: The Essential Writings and Speeches.* Ed. James M. Washington (HarperOne: 2003).

Moser, Whet. "A Brief History of Football Head Injuries and a Look Towards the Future." ChicagoMag.com. 5/4/12. Accessed 12/3/18. http://www.chicagomag.com/Chicago-Magazine/The-312/May-2012/A-Brief-History-of-Football-Head-Injuries-and-a-Look-Towards-the-Future/.

Plato. *Republic.* Transl. G.M.A. Grube (Hackett, 1992).

Rogers, Robert. "Robert Rogers' Standing Orders." GoArmy.com. Accessed 12/3/18. https://www.goarmy.com/ranger/about-the-rangers/rodgers-orders.html

Seneca. *Letters From a Stoic.* Transl. Robin Campbell (Penguin, 1969).

Sophocles. *Ajax.* Transl. R.C. Trevelyan. (Cornell University Library: 2009). http://classics.mit.edu/Sophocles/ajax.html

Stevens, John. *Budo Secrets: Teachings of the Martial Arts Masters.* Boston: Shambhala, 2002.

C

Weinberg, Rick. "Kerri Strug Fights Off Pain, Helps U.S. Win Gold." ESPN.com. June 29, 2008. Accessed November 30, 2018. https://web.archive.org/web/20080629004458/http://sports.espn.go.com/espn/espn25/story?page=moments%2F51

Whitehead, Alfred North. *Process and Reality* (Free Press, 1979).

J.C. Glick
LTC, U.S. Army, Retired

LTC (Ret) JC Glick is a leadership and culture consultant who advises at the strategic, operational, team and individual levels. He has a strong background in leadership development, executive personnel assessment and selection, strategy, coaching, counseling and developing innovative solutions to complex problems.

JC served in the U.S. Army as an infantry officer for 20 years, primarily in Special Operations and Special Missions Units with more than 11 combat tours. Since retiring from the military, JC has brought his innovative and unconventional thoughts on education, leadership and resiliency into the private sector, consulting with Fortune 500 companies, the NFL and professional sports teams including the Denver Broncos, the Carolina Panthers and the Charlotte Hornets.

JC recently wrote and published the thought-provoking, groundbreaking book titled "A Light in the Darkness: Leadership Development for the Unknown", which has been implemented by major corporations including the NFL and Microsoft and endorsed by leaders in the field of education, business and the military.

JC is considered a thought leader in adaptive and proactive programs of instruction centered on the development of leadership behaviors and values suited to dynamic environments and situations of ambiguity and adversity. JC recently developed the "Prodromos Developmental Model", a capacity-building system designed to develop people and leaders for the future, which is outlined in his first book. His methods have been featured in Forbes Magazine and the Huffington Post and his work has been referenced in Forbes, Inc. and Entrepreneur.

He is a graduate of the University of Rhode Island, holds a Master's Degree from the Naval War College and was a Senior Fellow in the Service Chief's Fellowship at the Defense Advanced Research Projects Agency (DARPA).

He has earned 3 Bronze Stars, 3 Meritorious Service Medals, a Joint Commendation Medal, and the Order of Saint Maurice. He is also an inductee of the University of Rhode Island ROTC Hall of Fame, as well as a Liberty Fellow, of The Aspen Institute and the Aspen Global Leadership Network

Dr. Alice Atalanta, Ph.D.

When Dr. Atalanta, an Ivy League graduate and single mom of two, found herself facing off in the amateur boxing ring against an opponent 15 years her junior—just released from prison for armed robbery--it was not what anyone in her former life would have expected. But Dr. Atalanta's life defies expectations, as she attacks the self-limiting beliefs that hold many women back.

A USA Boxing athlete, Dr. Atalanta is a single mom, sexual assault survivor, and sought-after commentator in the fight world on the topic of women's personal defense. She is a certified SPEAR System instructor with world-renowned combatives expert Tony Blauer, and she has also trained extensively with former Navy SEAL Dom Raso of Dynamis Alliance.

Dr. Atalanta holds a Ph.D., and two Master's Degrees from the University of Pennsylvania, as well as a Master's Degree from the University of Virginia, where she was an All-American athlete and snowboard team captain. She has extensive teaching experience at the collegiate and professional levels, having instructed at both universities as well as the Department of Veterans' Affairs. After completing her academic work, Dr. Atalanta directed her attention towards serving the Veterans' community, spearheading fundraising efforts for the SEAL Future Fund and Special Operations Warrior Foundation.

In addition to having written and published her own research on Aristotle's Ethics, Dr. Atalanta now specializes in working closely with writers from high-performance backgrounds. Her clientele runs the gamut from former Navy SEALs to the President of Floyd Mayweather's $100m Money Team brand. She has presented her own scholarship at Harvard University as well as various other academic conferences nationwide, and her work is currently featured in Havok Journal.